On
the
Banks
of
Jacobs
Creek

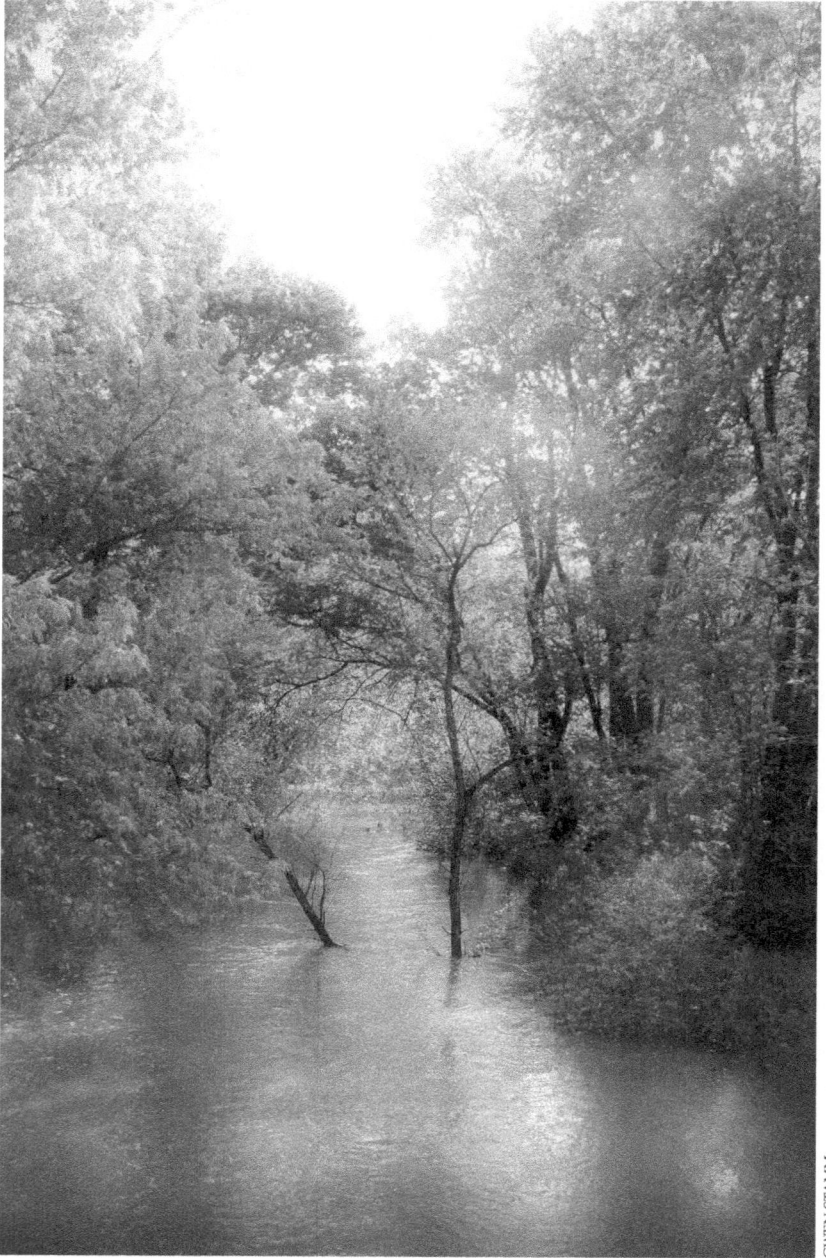

Jacobs Creek from Dexter Road, which connects North Scottdale and Kingview

On
the
Banks
of
Jacobs
Creek

A History of the
Scottdale Mennonite Churches

D ANIEL H ERTZLER

Foreword by
John E. Sharp

Scottdale Mennonite Church
Scottdale, Pennsylvania

Cascadia
Publishing House
Telford, Pennsylvania

Cascadia Publishing House orders, information, reprint permissions:
contact@CascadiaPublishingHouse.com
1-215-723-9125
126 Klingerman Road, Telford PA 18969
www.CascadiaPublishingHouse.com

On the Banks of Jacobs Creek
Copyright © 2018 by Cascadia Publishing House,
a division of Cascadia Publishing House LLC
Telford PA 18969
All rights reserved.
Library of Congress Catalog Number: 2018026171
ISBN 13: 9781680270112; ISBN 10: 1680270117
Cover and interior design by Gwen M. Stamm with cover photo
of Jacobs Creek as photographed by Gwen M. Stamm.

Library of Congress Cataloging-in-Publication Data
Names: Hertzler, Daniel, author. | Sharp, John E., 1951- writer of foreword.
Title: On the banks of Jacobs Creek : a history of the Scottdale Mennonite
    churches / by Daniel Hertzler ; foreword by John E. Sharp.
Description: Telford, Pennsylvania : Cascadia Publishing House, [2018] |
    Includes bibliographical references.
Identifiers: LCCN 2018026171| ISBN 9781680270112 (pbk. : alk. paper) | ISBN
    1680270117 (trade pbk. : alk. paper)
Subjects: LCSH: Scottdale Mennonite Church (Scottdale, Pa.)--History. |
    Mennonite Publishing House--History. | Mennonite Church--History. |
    Mennonite Church USA--History. | Scottdale (Pa.)--Church history.
Classification: LCC BX8131.S36 H47 2018 | DDC 289.7/74881--dc23
LC record available at https://lccn.loc.gov/2018026171

23 22 21 20 19   10 9 8 7 6 5 4 3 2

JACOBS CREEK begins on a farm near Acme, Pennsylvania, and ends at the town of Jacobs Creek on the Youghiogheny River. At Route 31 it becomes the border between Fayette and Westmoreland Counties. Kingview Church was in Fayette County, the North Scottdale and Scottdale Mennonite Churches in Westmoreland County.

The creek is named after Chief Jacob, "one of the Delaware chiefs who took up arms against Pennsylvania shortly after Braddock's defeat" (C. Hale Sipe, *Indian Chiefs of Pennsylvania* [1927; reprint, Lewisburg, PA: Wennawoods Publishing, 1994], 269). His name was assigned by Colonel Buchanan from near Lewistown "because of his close resemblance to a burly German in Cumberland County."

According to the account, Chief Jacob later resided at his cabin, not far from Mt. Pleasant in Westmoreland County, which is evidently why his name has been attached to the creek. A carved stone effigy of him is found above the creek, near the Laurelville Mennonite Church Center. Several websites give further reports.

From sources that I am not presently able to document, the chief's name was later designated as Captain Jacobs, and so references to the creek and to the town where it empties into the Youghiogheny River do not have an apostrophe but are simply Jacobs.

To all the volunteers in three Scottdale
Mennonite churches

Contents

Foreword: *By John E. Sharp* 11

Preface: *Why Should This Story Be Told?* 14

1 The Mennonite Church of Scottdale 17

2 The Kingview Story: How Does a Sunday
    School Become a Church? 30

3 North Scottdale: The Church in a Schoolhouse 42

4 North Scottdale and Kingview United:
    Merger and Pastoral Relations 55

5 Kingview Congregational Life 70

6 Mennonite Church of Scottdale: 1960–2003 88
    A Decade of Vigorous Activity: The 1960s 89
    A Decade of Change: The 1970s 95
    A Time to Do Church "Right": The 1980s 102
    Celebrations: The 1990s 109
    Beginning of the End: The 2000s 118
    The Closing of MPH and Its Effect
    on the Local Scene 121

7 Beginning Again in 2003 125

8 A Month of Sundays 136

What Happened to the Loucks Family?
By Daniel Hertzler 151

Pastoral Reflection: *By Donna Mast* 155

Appendixes: *Baptisms* 157

    1. Baptisms for Mennonite Church of Scottdale,
       1940–2003 158
    2. Baptisms for Kingview, 1952–2003 162
    3. Baptisms for North Scottdale, 1959–1969 164
    4. Baptisms for Scottdale Mennonite Church
       after Merger in 2003 165

The Author 166

Foreword

by John E. Sharp

DAN HERTZLER promises to write an honest account of the Mennonite presence in Scottdale, begun in 1790 and nearly fading out 100 years later. But pioneer evangelist John S. Coffman was encouraged by the talents of the faithful few who led a rebirth in 1893. The renewal spawned three congregations with a combined membership of 300 by midcentury, before dwindling once again to a single congregation of 50–75 attendees at the beginning of the twenty-first century.

An honest account means that Hertzler is candid about the upsides and downsides—the successes and weaknesses—of the people playing on this stage of history. The author traces the life and witness of the last half century, in which he himself was an actor, by using interviews, church bulletins, and board and committee minutes. As an astute observer and longtime writer and editor, Hertzler is well equipped to bring the complex pieces of this story to the stage.

Through its church-owned publishing ministry, begun in the early years of the twentieth century, Scottdale became the communication hub of the Mennonite Church, perched as it was at the western edge of the Allegheny Mountains. The influence of publishing was felt far and wide.

A favorite story in my family is that of our grandfather John S. Peachey, an Amish First World War draft counselor, who made repeated trips to Scottdale for the latest news from Washington, DC, affecting the experiences of conscientious objectors. As the story is told, after each consultation with Scottdale people, Peachey would return home with his clothes tucked under his arm and his suitcase filled with books. Thus the influence of Scottdale helped shape the worldview of the next generation in this Amish household.

The many who moved to Scottdale for its publishing ministry had the vision to build two additional congregations. Anchored by the main church on the hill, these congregations were spawned by robust outreach in the form of Sunday schools, Bible schools, revival meetings, and door-to-door evangelism. The new congregations began as Sunday schools, became independent congregations, and eventually merged. Kingview, the church in the valley, was organized in 1952, North Scottdale in 1959. Ten years later North Scottdale was absorbed into the Kingview Mennonite congregation. In 2003 Kingview and Mennonite Church of Scottdale merged to become the present Scottdale Mennonite Church.

Scottdale was fertile ground for progress and innovation. Local minister and editor Paul Erb was the chair of a newly formed churchwide Mennonite Youth Fellowship that was adopted in Scottdale in 1948. In the same year, church bulletins first appeared at the initiative of Kass Hernley. Writers and editors could test new teaching material in the local congregations. As they navigated the cultural changes that affected traditional Mennonite practice, leaders and members felt the scrutiny and the high expectations of the denomination.

The congregations faced conflict and, sometimes with difficulty, reached resolution. Most unsettling was the "dramatic and tumultuous" downsizing of the Mennonite Publishing House, a dominant feature of the business community since 1908. Unsurprisingly, this caused job loss, financial stress, distrust, severed relationships, pain and anguish. Perhaps most difficult was the apparent denunciation of many years of sacrificial service to the publishing ministry. Hertzler writes candidly about this traumatic series of events.

Taking the long view, one could mark the beginning of the decline in 1971, when a reorganized denomination began moving offices to Goshen and Elkhart, Indiana. But none of this indicated the

painful end, which came after another merger, that of the Mennonite Church and the General Conference Mennonite Church. New
leaders brought a strong critique of certain business practices that
had long sustained publishing. After significant downsizing, the
end of publishing in Scottdale came in 2011, when the remaining
operations were moved to Harrisonburg, Virginia. Three families,
deeply involved in the life of the congregation, followed the operations to Virginia, a further reduction in numbers.

The reduced membership of both congregations led to the
2003 merger of the Kingview and Scottdale congregations to create
the current Scottdale Mennonite Church. Hertzler points the way
forward with the congregation's vibrant membership covenant for
2017–18. There is still work to be done. ⟨⟨

> *March 3, 2018*
> *John E. Sharp*
> *History and Bible Professor*
> *Hesston College*

Preface

Why Should This Story Be Told?

THIS is the story of the Scottdale Mennonite Church, a congregation with a weekly attendance of 50 to 75 people in Scottdale, a town of some 5,000 in western Pennsylvania. Both church and town have colorful histories, some of the accounts more successful than others.

This will be an attempt to write an honest history of the church, to note the dedication that impelled these people's efforts while at the same time not ignoring factors that limited their effectiveness. The story of God's people has always included both of these factors, and the Mennonite story has had its own special features, especially its radical tradition. When all the other churches in town seem to follow Reinhold Niebuhr's position that "Jesus' way is not really for here and now," it might be expected that some who enjoy association would hesitate to join the Mennonite Church. And would the presentation be effective? What is an effective way of presenting this radical good news? Does it require more sacrifice than we were willing to give?

Mennonites have been in this area since 1790, as accounted by Edward Yoder in *The Mennonites of Westmoreland County, Pennsylvania* in 1942. By 1965 their membership was more than 300 members in three congregations, as described by D. Byron Yake in *Over the Alleghenies*, a historical booklet published in 1965.[1] How did the Scottdale Mennonites increase from a handful in 1893 to three congregations in 1965 and then decline to one small congregation in 2003?

In his account Edward Yoder describes the history in terms of three periods: (1) The Early Period, 1790–1840; (2) Middle Period, 1840–1892; (3) Recent Period, 1892–1940. He reports that the Early Period was a time of settling down, the Middle Period a time of decline, and the Recent Period a time of renewal beginning with the leadership of Aaron and Joseph Loucks.

The renewal involved a variety of features: (1) organizing a congregation in Scottdale, which eventually replaced the earlier Pennsville and Stonerville (later called Alverton) congregations; (2) beginning to teach the Bible in extension Sunday schools; and (3) the organization of the Mennonite Publishing House in 1908.

In 1940 the Scottdale Mennonite congregation seemed poised for an active future. There was a new meetinghouse built in 1939 on Market Street. Membership of the congregation was 170. There were two extension Sunday schools: East Scottdale, reestablished in 1920; and North Scottdale, started in 1934. Both met in local school buildings, with an enrollment of 136 in East Scottdale and around 100 in North Scottdale. "Both these extension Sunday schools seem to be filling a real need in the communities where they are held. They're not properly independent Sunday schools, but are conducted as extension schools of the Scottdale Mennonite congregation."[2]

Yoder comments on the source of increase in membership of the Scottdale congregation. "The greater part of the increase in the congregation's membership has come through members and their families who moved to Scottdale from other congregations of the Mennonite faith. Although there had been more than a century of Mennonite history and life in this vicinity before the present congregation was organized, the revived congregation has not been able to recover any appreciable number of those whose ancestors first brought the Mennonite faith into this section."[3]

It will be found that in the years following 1940, the dynamics of the Scottdale congregation were tied with and affected by the activities and expansion of Mennonite Publishing House. People moved here to work at MPH and were generally called on to work in the local church and Sunday school activities.

I want to give credit and thanks for the editorial work of David Garber. Every writer needs an editor, and Dave did the work.

Notes

1. Gerald C. Studer, ed., *Over the Alleghenies: The Coming of the Mennonites into Westmoreland and Fayette Counties, Pennsylvania* (Scottdale, PA: 175th Anniversary Committee, Scottdale Mennonite Church, 1965), 43.

2. Edward Yoder, *The Mennonites of Westmoreland County, Pennsylvania* (Scottdale, PA: Scottdale Mennonite Church, 1942), 58.

3. Yoder, *The Mennonites of Westmoreland County, Pennsylvania*, 54–55.

Also pertinent is Julia Spicher Kasdorf, "Planted by the Water: From Laurelville to Jacobs Creek, PA." She read it at Laurelville Mennonite Church Center on June 7, 2018. It is a personal and historical account of happenings in the Jacobs Creek area. Julia grew up here and has included a variety of personal experiences such as being bitten by a copperhead snake at Laurelville.

1

The Mennonite Church of Scottdale

THIS is an account of the Scottdale Mennonite Church, meaning the Market Street Mennonite Church or the Mennonite Church of Scottdale. All three of these names are found in the records, but the issue was settled by a June 12, 1956, "Constitution and Bylaws of the Mennonite Church of Scottdale, Market and Grove Streets, Pennsylvania."

It took the bulletin editor some time to catch up. On August 4, 1957, it is the Scottdale Mennonite Church, but on August 11 the Mennonite Church of Scottdale. However, the issue was still not completely settled. A bulletin note on September 6, 1959, says, "A number of individuals use the term 'Market Street Church' when referring to our congregation. Please note that the official name is 'Mennonite Church of Scottdale.'"

What was it like to be a member of this church in the 1940s and 1950s? It appears that the pattern of church activity described by Edward Yoder continued in the 1940s, but changes did come in the 1950s.

Notices of a semi-annual business meeting are found in a file, the first one dated 1939. But at first these records list only the names of committees, without copies of the reports. A January 25, 1940, document lists the names of 16 reports to be given at the meeting. Included here is a table of those 16 organizations scheduled to report:

Scottdale Mennonite Church, built in 1939

Church Reports to be Given on January 25, 1940
1. Charity Committee
2. YPBM [Young People's Bible Meeting] Committee
3. Prayer Meeting Committee
4. Cottage Prayer Meeting Committee
5. Tract Distributor
6. District Mission Board Member
7. Scottdale Mennonite Sunday School
8. East Scottdale Sunday School
9. North Scottdale Sunday School
10. Adult Sewing Circle
11. Intermediate Sewing Circle
12. Criterion Literary Society
13. Ministerial Body
14. Church Council
15. Church Building Committee
16. Board of Trustees

The leaders of East Scottdale and North Scottdale Sunday schools are included in the reporting. This indicates that these were considered major aspects of the congregation's ministry. A set of "Proposed Recommendations" presented on January 1, 1949, included the following: (1) "We recommend as an ultimate goal in our mission work that organized congregations be established with a full-time or part-time pastor and wife in charge. (2) That the Church Council continue to provide pastors for North and East Scottdale." How these recommendations were to develop will be described in the next two chapters.

SUPPLIED BY JOAN HORST

John L. Horst, 1929–1957

Leadership of the Scottdale congregation was stable in the 1940s. John L. Horst was pastor. The Global Anabaptist Mennonite Encyclopedia (GAMEO) reports that "in 1929 Horst was ordained by lot as pastor of the Scottdale Mennonite church, an unpaid position at that time." He served in that capacity until the mid-1950s, moving to Harrisonburg, Virginia in 1957.[1]

Serving as pastor had to be a marginal activity since Horst was employed at Mennonite Publishing House. However, he had considerable help with the preaching. A tally of his sermons found in the bulletins for 1948 showed only 14 times that he preached during that year.

Although records of business meetings seem to be lacking, notes of some collateral activities appear in the file. One of these was the Dorcas Sewing Circle, which had begun in 1918. The yearly report from April 1, 1945, to March 31, 1946, records 26 members with "71 garments made, 10 quilts, 42 comforters, 17 towels, and 900 pounds of used garments collected."

Milford Paul, Boys Club leader with Glenn Millslagle, one of the boys

There was also a Junior Sewing Circle. Minutes of the 38th meeting report that it "was held in the basement of the Mennonite Publishing House with 14 members and visitors present. Some of us mended church hymnals while others sewed. We finished 16 books."

Efforts to organize a Boys Club began in 1944. Glenn Millslagle remembers the Boys Club with its sponsors: Eugene Millslagle (his father), Orlo Brenneman, Ralph Hernley, and Milford Paul. "Miff Paul was the sponsor who spent the most time with us. We met every Monday evening at 6:00 o'clock at the YMCA for all kinds of games. . . . And then we would go swimming for the second hour. . . . We also used the summer months to play softball, football, and other games at the Jewell Loucks pasture field."

A major development in 1948 was the organization of a Mennonite Youth Fellowship (MYF). This was approached cautiously. A Church Council minute of May 12, 1948, reports an action, "That we approve the idea of the organization of a Mennonite Youth Fellowship and that the matter be brought before the congregation through a Young Peoples Bible Meeting program and possible action by the congregation."

On October 5, 1948, the Church Council reconsidered "the MYF Constitution, which had been referred back to the Fellowship Study Committee for clarification of various points. Paul Erb, chairman of this committee, called attention to the points that had been revised." The Council passed the following action: "That we approve the Mennonite Youth Fellowship Constitution."

It is of interest to note in *The Mennonite Encyclopedia*, "MYF was organized at Eureka, Ill., in 1948."[2] Paul Erb was author of the article. The beginning of Mennonite Youth Fellowship would affect the name of the Young Peoples Bible Meeting, but not until 1959. On February 24, 1959, the Council suggested "to the Church Constitution Revision Committee that the name of the Y.P.B.M. Committee be changed to the Sunday Evening Service Committee."

Bulletins for the Scottdale Mennonite Church began in 1948. They have been bound and provide specific information about church activities. One gets the impression that this was a very busy congregation. Weekly activities in the bulletin for February 27, 1949, were as follows:

Sunday Morning Service
    8:30   Teachers Meeting—C. F. Yake
    9:30   Sunday School—The Way of Love
  10:45   Review of the Lesson
  11:00   Sermon—J. L. Horst

Sunday Evening Service
    7:00   Reverence on the Lord's Day—Norma Hostetler
            Reverence in the Stewardship of Possessions—
            Lowell Hershberger
    8:00   Sermon—Millard Lind

Wednesday Evening Service
 7:30 Prayer Meeting—Ellrose D. Zook, leader
    Bible School
    Cottage Meeting
    Spenser Johnston—Kingview
    Washington Etling—Keifertown (East Scottdale)

In a survey of that month's bulletins, I find eight different preachers, all but one of them workers at Mennonite Publishing House.

The spiritual life of the congregation was enhanced by regular revival meetings. A Church Council minute from January 13, 1948, records, "The pastor reported that Jesse Short has been secured to conduct revival meetings from March 14 to 28." Tent meetings would be held near the Sunday schools. The same minute records that "the tent meetings will be held in East Scottdale from July 11 to 25 with C. C. Culp as evangelist."

At the East Scottdale Sunday school, begun in 1906 and opened again in 1920, and at North Scottdale, begun in 1934, many people seemed to enjoy the Sunday school classes for their own sake. But at least one family went beyond this and joined the Scottdale congregation. This was the Sterling Millslagles from East Scottdale. Glenn remembers "that we always headed to Market Street Mennonite as soon as Sunday school was over.

"The Brilhart family hired Dad to do odd jobs at their businesses and in their homes. When the coal mines were on strike or slow because of low demand, there just wasn't any money, and they could never get ahead working for coal companies. I remember Mom and Dad talking about Earl Brilhart recommending Dad to work for MPH. He was hired in 1947 or 1948, and our lives changed forever. MPH also loaned money to build our home on Oak Street in 1949. Mom always called it her dream house."

A concern developed to have more pastoral services than could be provided by a volunteer. On July 6, 1949, the Council decided to "recommend to the Business meeting that we request Bro. Horst to devote a portion of his time to pastoral work with a proportionate allowance. "On January 7, 1950, a Council minute reports that J. L. Horst declined this.

In 1949 action was taken to move the Sunday school at East Scottdale out of the schoolhouse and into its own building. A local businessman, Walter King, donated a parcel of land, and the building began. One can trace the progress of the building in bulletins of the Scottdale congregation throughout 1950 and 1951. The new building was dedicated in 1952. On February 1, 1953, "action was taken to authorize the solicitation of the congregation during February to reduce the indebtedness on the Kingview Church building, which stands at $7600." The same bulletin reported the membership of the Scottdale congregation at 258.

North Scottdale obtained a building by buying and remodeling the school building in which they met since East Huntingdon Township no longer needed it as a school building.

In the meantime the concern to have a pastor at Scottdale who was not employed at Mennonite Publishing House surfaced and was duly processed. Two meetings of the Church Council on January 11 and 14, 1954, presented several recommendations to the congregation.

1. That we reaffirm the express passed action of the Council and congregation that we should have a
   pastor who can give a major portion of his time to the work of the congregation with proportionate support.
2. The pastor should not be on the regular payroll of any other congregation except by consent of Church Council.

A special congregational meeting on January 28, 1954, basically affirmed these strategies, as reported in the January 31, 1954, bulletin.

In the meantime the Mennonite Church conducted summer Bible schools for the whole community, using local school buildings. On March 13, 1949, the bulletin reported that "the School Board has again granted permission for our Bible School in the Pittsburgh Street Building. Mr. Puff, superintendent of the Scottdale Public Schools, advises us that the School Board unanimously

Summer Bible School students in the Brilhart truck, June 1945, with C. F. Yake standing at right

agreed with me that the summer Bible school conducted by the Mennonite Church is a very good thing for the community." The school was held in the Pittsburgh Street school building, and similar schools were held in the East Scottdale and North Scottdale buildings.

In 1950 the bulletin reports Alta Mae Erb as director of the community-wide summer Bible school, with average attendance as 419 and classes at five places: Scottdale Mennonite Church, the Pittsburgh Street School, the Nazarene Church, East Scottdale School, and North Scottdale School.

In 1951 Alta Mae Erb is identified as director, with Ellrose Zook as principal at East Scottdale and Omar Stahl as principal

Alta Mae Erb, director of the community-wide Summer Bible School

at North Scottdale. Permission was also received to use the Chestnut Street School, and average attendance is reported as 480.8.

Plans to call an associate pastor are recorded in the bulletins. The bulletin for January 2, 1955, reports the presence of "Brother Willis Hallman and family over the weekend. . . . We are glad to learn to know them since there is a possibility that they may locate here sometime in the future." On February 13 it is reported that "at the special members meeting last Sunday afternoon, the recommendation to extend a call to Brother Hallman to be associate pastor of our congregation passed by 93 percent vote of those voting for or against the recommendation."

According to the February 27 bulletin, Brother Willis Hallman "states that he accepts the call as associate pastor of our congregation, beginning service in September." On September 25 it urges, "You will want to be present this evening for the dedication service when Brother Hallman will be installed as associate pastor."

The July 15, 1956, bulletin records that "by a vote of 87% Brother Willis Hallman was called to assume the full duties of pastor for a three-year term.

Willis Hallman, 1955–1959

SUPPLIED BY KATHERINE HALLMAN

The Hallmans have accepted this call. This service will be subject to review by the Board of Directors annually." Pastoral service, once assumed as traditional, is now to be directed by the Board.

At the same time there was concern about enlarging the Scottdale meetinghouse. A special business meeting on July 17, 1956, included minute 3: "That we enlarge the fund for building the education wing with regular offerings."

On July 17, 1958, reports to the Business Meeting include the

"Study Committee on Building Needs for Church and Sunday School." The report includes a ten-point task of the committee and states, "It was made clear that the committee is to examine every area of need, whether it is directly related to Christian education or not." At the second meeting of the committee "a list of church and Sunday school functions was made in an attempt to cover all areas of church activity for which there may be building needs." There follows a list of eight categories.

That the Scottdale Mennonite community was musically adept is illustrated by a December 22, 1957, announcement that "the traditional singing of the *Messiah* will be held at Milford Paul's at 9:30 PM New Year's Eve, December 31. Everyone who wishes to participate is invited."

North Scottdale eventually organized as a separate congregation. On January 26, 1958, it is reported in the bulletin, "We grant the request of the North Scottdale Church Council to organize as a separate congregation." It was also resolved "that we as the Scottdale congregation continue our financial support until the North Scottdale church building indebtedness is liquidated."

At the home congregation, stability was not to be taken for granted. On June 8, 1958, it is reported that "Willis Hallman has informed the Church Board that he is planning to go to school at the end of his period of service in August 1959."

The nature of Hallman's proposal is described in minutes of the Special Business Meeting on October 8, 1958. An option presented to the congregation would have "Willis Hallman serve as pastor for another three-year-term with the understanding that he would be attending school during the summers of 1959, 1960, 1961, and 1962." The minutes report that "the congregation decided by a majority vote in favor of calling someone else as pastor when the current three-year term of the pastor ends in September, 1959."

In 1959 attention was given to finding a replacement for Willis Hallman. Congregational minutes report that a vote was taken on a proposal to call Russell Krabill of Goshen, Indiana, as pastor. "On Sunday morning, June 14, Ben Cutrell announced that 90 percent of the voting members voted in favor of extending a call to the Russell Krabills to the pastorate."

On July 5, 1959, the bulletin reports that "for those who were not present on Sunday two weeks ago we repeat the announcement that Russell Krabill has declined a call to become pastor at Scottdale."

The qualifications for church membership appear as an issue in the records from time to time. On October 14, 1951, a full-page letter from "The Ministry" introduces the twice-yearly celebration of the Lord's Supper with a discussion of "two areas in Nonconformity to the World in which we need to guard ourselves are printed out in our "Rules and Discipline." The two are "Worldly Amusements" and "Pride in Apparel." Along with the letter is a four-point questionnaire to be returned on or before October 14.

On July 30, 1957, Willis Hallman "expressed the need for guidance on the question of church membership. He gave a list of those who worship with us who are not members. How to approach these people? It is difficult to give guidance to those who are not members." Some of the issues involved in the matter of church membership are women with cut hair and discipline for communion.

"A rather lengthy discussion followed in which it was pointed out that solving of these questions presents quite a challenge and poses a number of implications in view of the influence of our congregation among the brotherhood."

The Church Council Report for 1957 includes Item 4: "The question of church membership was discussed for some time. It was agreed that we favor accepting [women] members (who do not have long hair) at the discretion of the pastor and bishop."

On March 7, 1958, a minute of the Council notes as follows: "In respect to sharing the privileges of communion with believers not members of our congregation, Church Council did not see how the practice could be reduced to a fixed rule. The Council recommends that, as before, the bishop and pastor should be free to serve communion to such as they feel meet the qualifications for this spiritual sharing."

Urie Bender, Paul M. Lederach, A. J. Metzler, interim pastors

On July 17, 1958, the report of the bishop, A. J. Metzler, included the following:

> As in each generation, the changing Christian culture around us makes its impact upon us. Seeking the implications of the Scriptures in our lives and witness is a constant serious task. The position of our congregation in relation to our entire brotherhood calls for added caution in solving the problems of change within our pattern of church polity. We need to work closely with our conference in finding the Lord's answers to today's application of the Word.

The Extension Committee was among the committees reporting to the semi-annual meeting. On July 14, 1955, the following regular activities were reported: (1) Jail Service (Greensburg); (2) Rescue Mission (Pittsburgh), discontinued until further notice; (3) *The Way* distribution (Pittsburgh): "We have been told to stay off the streets with literature on penalty of a jail sentence." (4) Street Meetings: "We are thinking of trying to sponsor live Street meetings instead of recordings, especially during the summer"; (5) Hospital visitation. The Extension Committee also sponsored a Christmas display in several downtown store windows.

Reports in the file are regularly designated as "Semiannual Business Meeting." However, on December 16, 1958, "It was moved and passed that the January Business Meeting of the congregation be discontinued." The reporting seems to have anticipated this change, for a July 17, 1958, report is designated as "Annual Business Meeting." The July 15, 1959, meeting is similarly titled.

The Scottdale congregation continued looking inward to serve its own needs and outward to see what more could be done. In August 10, 1958, the bulletin carried an alert: "A questionnaire will be administered immediately after the morning service. Your opinions are needed to plan for a Sunday evening program that is designed to meet your needs." On September 27 it is noted that the "Mennonite Church of Scottdale is providing 22 of the 270 religious census takers." On January 18, 1959, the bulletin says, "The Extension Service Committee is making a study of nearby communities to consider a possible location for establishing a Sunday school."

In the meantime, pastoral transition proceeded apace. On August 2 we read, "Urie Bender has consented to serve as acting pastor on a temporary basis, during an interim when we will be without a pastor." So the Scottdale congregation was on a temporary basis with a part-time pastor who also worked at Mennonite Publishing House. As the 1960s approached, the daughter congregations were gaining a sense of stability. Meanwhile the mother church was without a regular pastor.〜

Notes

1. John L. Horst Sr. (1889–1964), from GAMEO: http://gameo.org/index.php?title=Horst,_John_L.,_Sr._(1889–1964).

2. *The Mennonite Encyclopedia* (Scottdale, PA: Mennonite Publishing House, 1957), 3:643.

2

The Kingview Story
How Does a Sunday School Become a Church?

THE East Scottdale Mennonite Sunday School began in a schoolhouse in 1906. With a two-year break from 1918 to 1920, it continued in schoolhouses until 1952, when the new meetinghouse was finished. In 1940 Edward Yoder wrote, "The East Scottdale Sunday school has exerted a wholesome influence on the children and youth of the community and has at the same time served as a training school in Christian work for numerous young people of the Scottdale Mennonite congregation."[1]

An early leader in this work was Martha Martin, who reported in *Gospel Witness*, one of the two publications that were later merged to become *Gospel Herald*. In addition to Sunday school, the ministry included books. Martin announced, "We bought a library of 51 books (a few more have been added), and since [then] quite a bit of visitation work has been done and much interest is being taken in the reading of these books." She also recounted having sold "two books, which were bought by a mother who had two boys in the penitentiary."[2]

When a new school was built, the Sunday school moved there also. The East Scottdale Sunday School was led by laypersons from the Scottdale Mennonite Church, assisted by ministers who preached occasionally and conducted evangelistic services (sometimes in a tent). In 1953 Ellrose D. Zook wrote an article for the *Southwestern Pennsylvania Conference News*, reflecting on the years as a Sunday school. He stated, "Perhaps between 50 and 100 souls

found their Savior
since the opening of
the work there. One
of these trophies of
grace was Richard
Teague, an old Eng-
lish miner who had
come to this coun-
try."[3] The article lists
the names of 11 Sun-
day school superin-
tendents and 12 evan-
gelists, illustrating

Frank and Anna Brilhart, leaders at East Scottdale (Kingview)

the combination of teaching and evangelistic preaching.

However, what Yoder reported in 1940 was still true: "Though numbers have attended the Sunday school for years, comparatively few from there have become active members of the Mennonite congregation."[4] The congregation, of course, was the Scottdale Mennonite Church.

Yet there were moves toward developing a more full-fledged organization in East Scottdale. The first was to supply a pastor. In 1947 Millard Lind was appointed by the Scottdale congregation to serve as pastor at East Scottdale. The next was to erect a building separate from the schoolhouse.

Walter King, a businessman, agreed to donate land for the building. He had attended the Sunday school as a child, although he never joined the Mennonite church. The new building was begun in 1950, dedicated at Easter 1952, and called Kingview.

As pastor at Kingview, Millard Lind, like John L. Horst at Scottdale, was employed full-time at Mennonite Publishing House and could not be expected to devote major time to building a congregation. So in 1953 Daniel Hertzler was employed part-time as assistant to the pastor, and Mabel Erb was recruited as church visitor, since visitation had been a significant part of the ministry from the beginning. Hertzler was an editor at Mennonite Publishing

DAVID HIEBERT

Kingview Mennonite Church, erected in 1949–50

House, and Erb was a clerk in the Mennonite Bookstore.

Hertzler left in 1954 to attend seminary at Goshen, Indiana, and Erb left for ministry in Puerto Rico. In the fall of 1954, Eugene Herr was called as assistant pastor. The congregation bought a house in Kingview as a parsonage. Eugene was soon married to Mary Yutzy, and the couple lived in the parsonage.

The bulletin on September 12, 1954, welcomed Eugene. His task was described as "visiting, preaching, sponsoring the youth fellowship, and assisting with administration of the work." Reviewing bulletins in the following weeks suggests that he took the youth work seriously.

On January 2, 1955, the bulletin announced a dedication meeting in the evening and stated, "While we have been operating as a congregation, yet officially we have been under Market Street Mennonite church. At tonight's meeting we become a separate congregation." Fifty-nine persons signed the charter membership sheet, one-third of them from the Kingview area. At the beginning of writing this history, however, only 3 of the 59 were continuing as members of the present Scottdale Mennonite congregation: Arlene

ANABAPTIST MENNONITE BIBLICAL SEMINARY

Millard Lind, 1949–1955, 1957

Miller, and Daniel and Mary Hertzler. The rest have either moved away, died, or ceased affiliation. Arlene remembers that when they came to Scottdale, they chose Kingview because her husband, Mervin, said, "The acoustics made singing so enjoyable," and she "chose Kingview because of Millard Lind's Sunday school class." Mary Hertzler died in November 2017, and Arlene Miller moved to Indiana in 2018. Hence, of the 59 charter members, "I alone am left" (1 Kings 19:14).

Numbers of adults at Kingview found the Sunday school activities quite satisfying and evidently saw no need to become members of the congregation. The Men's Bible Class and the King's Daughters had social activities in addition to the Sunday school classes.

The January 2, 1955, bulletin and those following show an active congregational program, with morning and evening services plus youth and children's activities. An evening service on March 6 was a panel discussion on prayer, with presentations by six persons. During the week of April 24 to May 1, evangelistic services were held in the church. Abner Miller, from the Mennonite congregation in Cumberland, Maryland, was the evangelist. Each evening one special group in the congregation would be addressed by the evangelist.

On May 1, 1955, Millard Lind resigned as pastor. He mentioned that in the time he was pastor "a church building has been erected, a full church program has been inaugurated, and the congregation established. Indeed, the Lord has so blessed the work that we have come to where we unitedly feel that the pastor must put major time into the work." His successor would be Eugene Herr. On June 5 the morning message was "The Pastor's Business," by the pastor, a sign that Eugene was now on duty.

Eugene's work with young people continued. The Sunday evening program on November 6 of 1955 addressed the theme "The Christian's Armor," presented by nine young

Eugene Herr, 1954–1957

MENNONITE CHURCH USA ARCHIVES

people, with a final talk by the pastor. The nine young people were Kenneth Dugger, Ruby Vernon, Bertha Hollis, Elva Mae Hebenthal, Edgar Lynn, Ruth Echard, Jean Goshorn, Wilma Vernon, and James Dewalt. None of these nine young people remained with Kingview church until the merger of 2003. A recent effort to check on their whereabouts found the following information: Kenneth Dugger and Bertha Hollis Sirianni had died, Edgar Lynn moved to New York state, James Dewalt to Ohio, Jean Goshorn to Chicago (we think), Ruby Vernon Stull to Vanderbilt. Ruth Echard has married, and the whereabouts of the others are unknown. Their stories illustrate a problem Kingview has had as a congregation: difficulty finding numbers of persons who would remain with the congregation. However, there were always some who would become faithful members.

Bulletins throughout 1956 show a vigorous program, and on November 11, 1956, there was an anniversary program to commemorate 50 years since the beginning of the East Scottdale Sunday School. In honor of this occasion, Anna G. Blackburn, a longtime attendant who never became a member, wrote a song titled "Red Chapel in the Valley," to be sung to the tune of the "Little Brown Church in the Vale."[5]

The anniversary was followed by a weeklong missionary conference, with speakers representing nine different mission efforts in eight foreign countries.

Kingview church ended 1956 with a vigorous church program. Something was provided for just about every age group. But change was on the way. Eugene Herr had not been able to finish his theological education before taking the Kingview assignment. On Sunday evening, June 2, 1957, there was a Farewell Service for Eugene and Mary Herr. No pastor's name appeared in the June 16 bulletin, but summer Bible school did begin the next day.

So the congregation began the search for another pastor. It was generally understood that Eugene Herr had inherited income and was able to get along with the very modest salary provided by the church. It was not expected that another pastor would be so "blessed," and so Kingview and North Scottdale (a mile away) agreed to work together on pastoral support, each one expecting half-time pastoral services.

It was discovered that Edwin Alderfer would consider this assignment, although he would not be available until 1958 because at that time he was assistant superintendent of Christopher Dock Mennonite High School at Lansdale, in Eastern Pennsylvania. The two congregations agreed to wait. The September 29, 1957, bulletin reports, "Both North Scottdale and Kingview have voted to call Edwin Alderfer as pastor of the two churches, to be available as soon as possible next year."

In the meantime Millard Lind was asked to serve as acting pastor until Alderfer could arrive. His name first appears in the bulletin for October 6, 1957. On October 29 it is reported that Edwin Alderfer had officially responded to the invitation to become pastor at Kingview and North Scottdale. However, he reminded the churches "that a pastor and his family are only one unit of a congregation." It was a concern that would surface from time to time after his arrival. The two congregations sent the Alderfers a turkey as a Christmas gift.

The parsonage where the Herrs had lived was too small for a family with four children. It was agreed that Kingview should provide a parsonage. On March 10, 1958, a representative group from the Kingview congregation voted to build a parsonage. With the combination of hired and volunteer work, the parsonage was finished in late July, and the Alderfers moved in. In the August 3, 1958, bulletin the Alderfers thank the congregation for "making such a lovely residence available to us." On the same date Edwin Alderfer's name appears in the bulletin as pastor. He was ordained to the ministry at North Scottdale on August 24 and installed at Kingview on August 31. Now he was pastor of two congregations one mile apart.

The schedule for his attendance at the two services was arranged as follows:

> 1st Sunday of the month at both places
> 2nd Sunday at Kingview
> 3rd Sunday at both places
> 4th Sunday at North Scottdale
> 5th Sunday at both places

What difference would it make to have a regular pastor after a year without one? Church activities continued much as before, but questions were raised from time to time about issues of faithful Christian living and evangelistic outreach. These appeared in minutes of the Church Board or annual congregational meetings. There was now a pastor who was expected to stay for a while and so would have a long-range perspective.

Occasionally these concerns spilled over into the bulletins. On December 7, 1958, the bulletin reported a Church Board discussion on the need for intercessory prayer in the congregation. The Church Board moved to encourage the pastor to enlist prayer partners who would participate in this ministry with him. It issued a challenge:

"Please volunteer for this ministry by contacting the pastor."

On May 18, 1959, the pastor issued a prophetic statement to the Church Board. "We are not an integrated congregation with clearly defined goals. Individual groups within the congregation are doing their work, but there may be little relation to the whole." In handling this issue, the board members agreed to personally respond to the following questions: "(1) What is our congregation's task? (2) What are the major obstacles which prevent accomplishing our congregational objectives?"

On June 1 the Church Board secretary listed three statements on the identity of the church, 14 statements on the functions of the church, and ten statements on obstacles to efforts to accomplish these objectives. The two lists are wide ranging and might well serve as the agenda for study of the church. But the Church Board was not an administrative group, and no evidence appears that these 24 statements were ever applied to any of the church programs. However, numbers nine and ten seem of interest: "(9) close relationships of a large bloc of members which distinguishes the bloc from others; (10) constantly entertaining nonmembers at regular church services." In other words, some of the Sunday school mentality still prevailed.

Frank Brilhart had been a longtime worker at the East Scottdale Sunday School and was a member of the building committee for the "Red Chapel in the Valley." He was also a member of the Church Board at the time of the meeting described above. All the other members represented the next generation and were employees of Mennonite Publishing House.

In 1959–61, Rodney Cavanaugh, a young member of the congregation, did I-W alternative service at Norristown (Pa.) Mental Hospital. When interviewed in 2015 for the Scottdale *Independent Observer*, he remembered having done entrance interviews at the hospital there. This was a challenge since these people were certainly not interested in entry. Other Mennonite young men from Scottdale and North Scottdale did alternative service.[6]

On June 12, 1960, the minutes of the Church Board report that "a large part of our time was spent discussing our need for more intimate communication among ourselves and also with other people who are not members. . . . Together as a Board we ask God's forgiveness and guidance in the future."

Beginning in 1960 there were annual congregational reports. Each person responsible for a significant part of the congregational program was supposed to write a statistical report. The pastor would add some visionary comments to his report. In 1963 he wrote, "You are to be commended for your continuing readiness to work diligently at being the church. This has required much time and energy for a number of you in the face of personnel and financial shortages." On the other hand, "Some areas of our congregational life that continue to need attention are evangelism, prayer, organizational structure, and administrative procedures; our present activity program, our purpose as a congregation, our responsibilities as a congregation, our relationships within the congregation, and relationships to the Kingview-Keifertown community." Surely a comprehensive list of pastoral concerns.

In 1965 the Kingview congregation accepted a new constitution. The pastoral report for that year commented on this favorably but observed, "Our major energy now will not need to be in structure. It remains for us to give ourselves to fulfilling our mission as a congregation in both its local and universal aspects."

The new constitution provided for several new roles: (1) a director of education and (2) elders. The reports appear in the 1965 annual compilation. The director of education observed that "changing the organization (such as the addition of a Christian education director) will not necessarily improve the quality of our education unless it can make possible (1) increased vision for the work so that we can take it more seriously and (2) improved skills so we are able to educate more effectively."

The report of the elders suggested that they were feeling their way into their assignment. More significant action would come later.

The minutes of the 1965 congregational meeting indicate in-

Edwin Alderfer, 1958–1969

terest in a change of emphasis in the pastor's ministry, from the pastor doing a lot of community visitation to the pastor "preparing the members to do this type of work." It is remembered that lay ministry was a longtime emphasis at East Scottdale (Kingview). A new generation may have been relaxing too much since now there was a pastor.

A note on this meeting indicates that the pastor had asked congregational permission to wear a conventional suit in place of a traditional Mennonite "plain coat." Action was taken at the meeting that "Edwin be granted the privilege of wearing a conventional suit, not only during the week, but also at our worship services."

Through the middle and the late years of the 1960s, several items of concern on how to be a church emerged: (1) how to be faithful as practicing Christians, (2) who to invite to the Lord's Supper, (3) effective outreach, and several new ones: (4) the request of the pastor for a year's leave of absence, and (5) the North Scottdale dilemma since termite damage had been found in their meetinghouse, a former school building.

What appears to be a significant document is Exhibit A to the October 15, 1968, Annual Business Meeting. It reports that on January 1, 1968, a congregational statement had been adopted, which began, "We believe that as individual Christians we need the help of all members of the congregation in discerning the will of the Holy Spirit as to how we may present our bodies as living sacrifices to Christ."

Then follow statements on these topics: (1) hair and veiling,

(2) jewelry and attire, (3) alcohol and tobacco, (4) mass media and dancing. The opening statement recognizes "that social customs and conditions will change and that the Christian's outward practices will vary as [each believer] expresses . . . Christian ideals in the current social setting."

The statements seek to recognize the various ambiguities involved in responding to social practices, but they tend to support what might have been considered traditional Mennonite nonconformity. On alcohol, the statement recognizes a certain openness in the Scriptures but expresses the belief that "total abstinence is the best choice for the Christian."

Within a year the statement on hair and veiling was to be tested. The December 27, 1968, minutes of the Elders ask, "In light of the statement adopted by the congregation urging the wearing of the prayer veiling during worship, what is the responsibility of the elders when this is ignored?"

On March 23, 1969, Edwin Alderfer asked for a year's leave of absence to attend the School of Pastoral Care at Winston-Salem, North Carolina. The Elders recommended and the Executive Committee approved "a one-year leave of absence from July 1, 1969, to June 30, 1970." The congregation would make interim arrangements for pastoral services during this period.

In the meantime, North Scottdale, which had become a congregation in 1959 but had discovered termite destruction in its building bad enough to conclude that the building could not be saved, contacted Kingview about the possibility of merger. On September 11, 1968, the Kingview Executive Committee received a report from Paul Erb indicating that "North Scottdale Council is recommending a favorable reply to our invitation to work toward a merger of our two congregations. . . . Along with this, they are recommending that North Scottdale cease to function as a congregation, October 1, 1969."

Beginning on July 12, 1970, Edwin Alderfer's name appeared in the bulletin as pastor of the merged congregation.⟲

Notes

1. Edward Yoder, *The Mennonites of Westmoreland County* (1940), 54.

2. Martha Martin, *Gospel Witness*, date uncertain.

3. Ellrose D. Zook, "Sunday School for 45 Years, Now Kingview Mennonite Church," in *Southwestern Pennsylvania Conference News* (March–April, 1953).

4. Yoder, *The Mennonites of Westmoreland County, Pennsylvania, 54.*

5. "Red Chapel in the Valley," by Anna G. Blackburn.

> There's a new red chapel in the valley,
> The dream of its people come true;
> This dear red chapel in the valley
> Lies between the hills of Kingview.
>
> There we will all meet to worship
> Together on each Sabbath Day,
> O come, let us walk together
> And offer our praises and pray.
>
> *Chorus*
> O, come, come, come, come.
> Come to this chapel in the valley
> And worship with folks there too.
> O come to this chapel in the valley
> That lies 'tween the hills of Kingview.

6. Scottdale's *Independent Observer*, April 30, 2015.

3

North Scottdale
The Church in a Schoolhouse

THE North Scottdale Mennonite Sunday School began in 1934 and continued until 1969, when the congregation merged with the Kingview Mennonite Church. The date of beginning is confirmed by an April 7, 1958, letter from J. Irvin Brunk to C. F. Yake. He remembered that "the first session was held the first Sunday in July 1934."

Brunk recalled further that "the Scottdale church furnished us with the songbooks and the first quarter's supplies. After that we were self-supporting and gave the regular missionary offerings." He also reported, "The women's class had organized meetings soon after the Sunday school began, and they were a highlight once a month for the women. . . . I was superintendent from the beginning till June 1946, when we left for California. A building fund was started several years before we left."

There was still a close tie to the home congregation designated as "Market Street." Their services would be listed in the North Scottdale bulletin, and on April 18, 1954, people were invited to evangelistic meetings at Market Street with George R. Brunk preaching. Transportation was provided, and a week later it was reported that the following had made decisions for Christ: "Milton and Margaret Hollis, Martha Lint, and Annabel Guptill." Sunday school attendance on October 9, 1955, was 110, and on December 16 it was 120. On January 22, 1956, the bulletin recognized 28 persons for perfect attendance during the last quarter of Sunday school.

North Scottdale, 1934–1969

Bulletins appear in the file beginning in 1952. J. Irvin Brunk's view of the women's class is confirmed by a bulletin note on November 22, 1953: "On Thursday evening the King's Daughters enjoyed a tour through the Publishing House and then went to Myrtle Yingling's for a Thanksgiving meeting. The offering of dimes for Korea and Jordan amounted to $28.25." A minute book in the file records meetings of this group from January 31, 1955, through December 16, 1966.

A Sunday morning program on January 3, 1954, suggested personal and congregational determination:

I Want to Forget the Sins and Failures of the Past —
    Florence Ridenour
Poem — Janet Walsh
I Want to Know Christ Better — Wendell Stants
Poem — Bertha Hollis
I Want to Be a Better Christian — Hugh Utterback
Bible mottoes for 1954 — Congregation
Special music by a sextette

Ownership of the school building was obtained in 1954. A carbon copy of a July 7, 1954, letter from the Scottdale congregation Board of Trustees indicates that they submitted a bid of $3,005 "for the North Scottdale property having an area of about 1 acre of land and having thereon erected a three-room frame building." A July 8 letter from Arthur F. Green, Supervising Principal, affirms, "You were awarded the North Scottdale property at your bid of $3,005 at a meeting of the Board of Education, July 7, 1954." A note in

Ruth Brunk with her husband, J. Irvin Brunk, first superintendent of North Scottdale Sunday school

SUPPLIED BY DALE BRUNK

the Scottdale Mennonite bulletin for July 7, 1954, reports that "all furnishings . . . were purchased earlier at the bid of $237.25."

Herbert Weaver remembers that "when we first met at North Scottdale, the building was still used as a school. We sat in the small desks that the students used. Some of us didn't fit very well." He also recalls, "After the building was not used as a school, we took out the partition between the two large rooms and put up a heavy curtain. That could be moved aside for church and put in place for Sunday school."

Beginning in 1948 the bulletins of Scottdale Mennonite Church report the appointment of pastors at Kingview and North Scottdale on a six-month basis. On August 1, 1948, the bulletin records the appointment of Harold Brenneman as pastor at North Scottdale. The January 23, 1949, bulletin reports "that we accept the resignation of Harold Brenneman as pastor at North Scottdale and that Paul Erb be appointed as pastor for the next six months, subject to his acceptance."

PAUL M. SCHROCK

Paul Erb, 1951–1956

Evidently he accepted because on January 12, 1951, the bulletin reports the appointment of "Paul Erb as pastor, with L. S. Weber as assistant, for another six months." The July 29 bulletin does not mention a reappointment. However, it notes that "we hope to distribute a digest of actions taken." It appears that reappointment was one of those actions. According to the August 5 bulletin, Paul Erb was preaching at North Scottdale.

The North Scottdale bulletins begin on October 19, 1952, with L. S. Weber preaching. Throughout the next several years Paul Erb and L. S. Weber are found preaching regularly. Between June 20, 1954, and October 2, 1955, there are no bulletins in the file. But on the latter date the bulletin reports that Paul Erb was installed as pastor, and on November 6 his name appears in the bulletin as pastor.

This continues until February 1956, when Paul Erb is listed as pastor with Willis Hallman (pastor at Scottdale Mennonite Church) as associate pastor. Beginning on October 14, 1956, Willis Hallman is listed as pastor and then in 1958 as acting pastor. On July 17, 1958, Edwin Alderfer is listed as pastor, a half-time supported assignment, with the other half supported by Kingview.

There seems to be no report on what these pastors may have done more than preaching. Yet the records show that after Edwin Alderfer became pastor, more pastoral work was being done than only preaching.

A dedication of the North Scottdale Mennonite Church, held on April 20, 1958, included an address by C. F. Yake, "Hitherto Hath the Lord Helped Us," and "Reminiscences by Early Sunday School

Scholars." The prayer of dedication was led by Willis Hallman, the acting pastor who had begun at North Scottdale in addition to his role as pastor at Scottdale Mennonite Church. Earlier pastors appointed by the Scottdale congregation had included Harold Brenneman and Paul Erb. The program also lists "Future Pastor: Edwin Alderfer (after July 1.)" Beginning on July 27, Edwin Alderfer is listed in the bulletin as pastor. Edwin would serve the congregation half-time, with the other half devoted to the Kingview congregation.

Recognition by Allegheny Mennonite Conference as a congregation separate from the Scottdale church came on May 3, 1959, with an endorsement by Paul M. Lederach and Paul E. Bender. Fifty-four persons comprise the charter membership list. Five of them are now (as of May 2018) members of the Scottdale Mennonite Church: Winifred Paul, Jim and Jane Sprinkle, Nancy Sprinkle Keyser, and Herbert Weaver.

VIRGIL YODER

North Scottdale charter members now at Scottdale Mennonite Church: Herbert Weaver, Nancy Keyser, Jane and Jim Sprinkle; Winifred Paul (at right), who died June 1, 2018

PAUL M. SCHROCK

The record from bulletins and organizational minutes is enhanced by personal memories, especially those of James Sprinkle, who grew up in this congregation. As Jim recalls it, his parents, Jesse and Ruth, were members at Scottdale Mennonite Church. They had been married by John L. Horst in 1936, and Ruth transferred her membership from the Lutheran Church. But for

Ruth and Rhoda Ressler, who began to take the Sprinkle children to North Scottdale

some reason Jesse began to wear a mustache, and the Scottdale congregation saw this as a military symbol.

He was forbidden to attend church with a mustache, and so the family dropped out of church for four or five years. Then Ruth and Rhoda Ressler, who later became missionaries to Japan, began to take the Sprinkle children to the North Scottdale Sunday School, and the family eventually came to North Scottdale. Jesse shaved his mustache and began to wear a Mennonite "plain coat."

Reading bulletins and other records from the 1950s and early 1960s, one finds a Sunday school and emerging congregation serious about the practice of the Christian faith and concerned to share it with others. The May 23, 1954, bulletin announces, "All those who recently accepted Christ and all those who desire to study together the essentials of the new birth, the way to victory, and fellowship in the church, meet with Raymond Wenger in one of the other rooms during the preaching service."

The earnestness is demonstrated in bulletin notes from time to time. For example, the twice-yearly observance of the Lord's Supper was taken very seriously. On May 7, 1959, the spring communion service is announced for May 24, and all members are asked to return their communion letters to the pastor by Friday. On November 1, 1959, the bulletin announces that November 15 is the date for communion, and the pastor is planning to visit all the members before that time. On November 15 it is reported that "due to several public events in the church and the community, it has been impossible for the pastor to visit all the members before the communion service. He will, however, continue his visits after communion in an attempt to visit those who were missed." Attendance was taken at communion. The April 10, 1960, bulletin reports that 46 persons were at communion last Sunday evening. Seventeen members were absent.

There was a youth fellowship, and a note on October 25, 1959, indicates that "the North Scottdale and the Kingview MYFs each voted to become the NSK-MYF. This has come as a result of both MYF groups having been so small that it was difficult to have helpful and meaningful MYF programs and activities." Activities of the NSK-MYF were listed from time to time in bulletin notes.

On February 7, 1960, the Sunday Evening Committee stated its aims "to plan for services on the second and fourth Sundays of the month, but [be] free to change the schedule to serve the best interests of the congregation." On November 27 it was announced that December 4 would be the first study in *God Leads Us to Witness at Home*, by A. Grace Wenger. "Get a copy before then. Chapters 1, 2, 3, and 6 will be for use in preparation for Spiritual Renewal meetings in January."

There were regular reminders of the mission of the congregation. On June 4, 1961, it was stated that "winning others to Christ through the Sunday school requires efforts of class members as well as the teachers. Are you willing to let the Holy Spirit use you in bringing others to Christ? Are you praying that someone will open his heart to the Lord?"

Personal Bible readings were announced in the bulletins. They seem too extensive to expect anyone to follow them. On May 22 they are Hebrews and James. On July 17, the Gospel of Mark; on July 31, Luke; and on August 21, the Gospel of John. Fast readers could do these, but in a congregation not all are fast readers. Herbert Weaver said he did not remember this program. The November 12, 1961, bulletin announces that "beginning with Thanksgiving Day the Bible reading program will correspond to that outlined by the American Bible Society around The Word for The World. Copies of this reading schedule are on the table."

As at Kingview, the congregation considered a group of specific cultural practices traditionally seen by Mennonites as aspects of Christian faith. Church Council minutes for March 22, 1960, report that "some questions were raised about our life and conduct as a church, such as wearing apparel, jewelry, drinking, etc., and what our attitude should be toward them. Brother Alderfer suggested that we examine the Allegheny Conference Discipline and basic doctrine through sermons and midweek discussions."

On May 31, 1960, "there was further discussion among the Council regarding the conduct of the Christian life. The discussion was in light of the Allegheny Conference rules of the church. Members were requested to read and acquaint themselves with the rules and discipline."

On February 4, 1962, the bulletin reports that "Change in Our Church Life will again be the theme of our midweek discussion. The focus this week will be on cut hair for women and the use of the devotional veiling." On February 18 it is reported that "under the direction of our bishop, brother A. J. Metzler, our three Scottdale congregations and the Masontown congregation will begin a study of two questions: (1) What is the basis for membership in the church? (2) What is the basis for participation in the communion service? . . . How can we be a disciplined church and then be free of legalism?"

A July 11, 1962, report by Ivan Moon, chair of the Church Council, presented two statements related to church membership and participation in communion:

We approve the principle that the needs of the individual are to be served rather than the maintenance of a hard and fast rule.

We are satisfied with the statement presented on the qualifications both for communion and for membership.

However, we express a concern that these statements should not be interpreted [to mean] that the congregation has no responsibility for the maintenance of a disciplined church.

On October 24, 1965, it is reported that "Council granted . . . Pastor Alderfer's request to wear a conventional suit."

The Sunday school evidently taught the Mennonite peace position, and four young men got the message. Their entry into I-W civilian service is reported in the following bulletins: Jim Sprinkle, July 29, 1956; Wendell Stants Jr., June 7, 1959; Gilbert Ridenour, October 8, 1961; Jerry Sprinkle, May 15, 1966. Two others are reported as having entered the Air Force: Hugh Utterback, June 7, 1959; and David Hershberger, December 29, 1963.

Jim Sprinkle remembers one more: Richard Walsh, who joined the Air Force but would come back to visit "the Mennonites" from time to time. Jim says that after he retired from the Air Force, Walsh moved to Farmington, New Mexico, and joined the Mennonite congregation there. He became ill, and the pastor and his wife, Aden and Edith Gingerich, took him into their home and cared for him until he died.

There is a file of annual congregational reports beginning in 1960. Most extensive are the reports of Edwin Alderfer, the pastor. As with Kingview, his reports include commendations and concerns. In 1959–60 he said, "Your cooperation and response as a congregation has been an encouragement and a challenge to me. When opportunities for service, witness, and testimony have been clearly set before you, you have always responded with a loving spirit and a ready heart."

On the other hand, he points out challenges:

There are several areas of concern that I would invite your attention to so that we might together work at them under the leading of the Holy Spirit: the poor attendance at mid-week services; the growing number of persons who attend only for Sunday school or for church; the frequency with which Sunday school classes are left without a teacher; the fact that a number of members are unoccupied in the regular work of the church; the fact that we haven't been able to hold the young people and to attract new ones; the need to improve

Edwin Alderfer, 1958–1969

SUPPLIED BY FAITH ALDERFER

the appearance of our building and grounds; the need for a young married people's fellowship.

"But," he also writes, "as a family we are grateful for your loving concern, prior support, material provisions, and warm fellowship." These were the ups and downs of a pastoral perspective.

On July 11, 1962, the pastor writes, "There has been considerable growth in our congregational life this year," and he follows with ten evidences. The first is "increased love towards and acceptance of one another," and the tenth is "growth both in understanding and experiencing the work of the Holy Spirit." The list, of course, is followed with a number of suggestions.

Space would fail to report the vision of all the leaders who were featured in these reports. However, in 1962–63 the Sunday school superintendent, James Sprinkle, commented, "To my knowledge the attendance has held pretty much the same over the last three quarters. This, I think, is mainly because of the faithfulness and hard work of the teachers, as they take an earnest interest in interpreting the lesson to the pupils."

On July 30, 1964, the ushers wrote, "We deemed it a privilege to serve as ushers this past year. We have tried to carry out our re-

sponsibilities to the best of our abilities and to the glory of God."
The ushers were Tony Ramos, Carl Keyser, Jerry Sprinkle, and
Philip Paul.

Beginning in the mid-1960s questions are raised about the purpose of the congregation. After mentioning the need for repairs to
the church building in his 1967 report, Edwin Alderfer wrote, "It
seems to me that we have not yet fully answered the question 'What
is our reason for being a congregation at this place?'" The names
of 72 members are included in his report for that year. A year later
it was 62. That year Herbert Weaver, chair of the trustees, reported:

> The trustees were instructed by the Church Council to con-
> duct a physical survey of the church building to determine
> how much termite damage there has been to the building and
> also to try to determine what condition the roof and siding
> are in. This was done and the report given to the Church
> Council at a combined meeting of the North Scottdale and
> Kingview congregations.

An undated one-page comment from Paul and Alta Erb is titled, "On the North Scottdale Situation." It states:

> We have been glad to be a part of this work. If problems con-
> cerning our building had not arisen, we see no argument for
> discontinuing the work here. . . . We do not favor anything
> less than the full program of repair which was earlier pre-
> sented to the church. We should count on this costing $10,000.
> . . . It is our prayer that a true spirit of Christian brotherhood
> may be manifested in whatever steps we take."

The May 21, 1967, bulletin announces, "The Church Council
has recommended that Brother Erb and Pastor Alderfer arrange a
meeting for counsel with other brethren from our sister Scottdale
congregations on the question of the future of our congregation."

However, congregational activities continued. On January 28,
1968, a 5:00 p.m. congregational supper at the church is announced:

"Remember, each family is to prepare to dramatize a verse that helps families to live happily together. The others will guess the truth acted out."

On January 14, 1968, the bulletin says, "Keep your schedules open for a joint meeting with Kingview the Sunday afternoon of February 11." The February 11 bulletin stresses the importance of all members being present for that afternoon meeting. "Nonmembers are also welcome. From this meeting should come direction for our future congregational life."

On April 28 a meeting is reported that discussed the future of the three Scottdale congregations: "In light of the proposed closing of the N[orth] Scottdale building, we all need to be thinking of forward steps of the Mennonite program for Scottdale." There would be one or two congregations, assuming that North Scottdale would cease.

On May 12, 1968, it is announced that "Jess Sprinkle, Ivan Moon, Carl Keyser, and Herbert Weaver will be available after the service to receive your returns on the way you feel would be best for the Mennonite churches in Scottdale to be formed."

On Sunday, June 23, 1968, the bulletin states: "In view of the interest shown on the questionnaires for continuing our congregation at this place, the Church Council has asked Paul Erb, Jess Sprinkle, and Edwin Alderfer to suggest possible ways this might be done."

On September 22, 1968, the bulletin reports a recommendation of the Church Council, which had been adopted at the September 15 congregational meeting. It responded favorably to an invitation from the Kingview congregation to work toward one congregation. The second point resolved "that we continue our present program at North Scottdale until October 1, 1969."

This action was confirmed by a two-thirds majority of those present at the meeting. "This vote was 18 yes and nine no, an exact two-thirds majority. The 27 votes cast were 58.5 percent of the resident membership of 46. The 18 votes in favor of the recommendation were 39 percent of the resident membership." The congregation would continue for another year under this cloud.

On January 5, 1969, Herbert Weaver and Mrs. Lowell Hershberger are announced "to serve on the Committee on Merger. The committee will be responsible to suggest ways for Kingview and our congregation becoming one by October 1, 1969."

On March 7, the bulletin announced: "A time of prayer in behalf of the North Scottdale–Kingview unity committee and its work . . . is being held weekly on Tuesdays at 12:30 p.m. at the Ivan Moon residence."

On May 4, 1969, a congregational meeting was held "to get the response of the congregation by ballot to the plan of the Unity Committee for combining the Kingview congregation with ours." On May 11 the results of the voting are reported: yes, 25; no, 5. Incomplete ballots, 6.

On June 22 there was a farewell for the Alderfer family since Edwin would be leaving for a year of training at North Carolina Baptist Hospital's Department of Pastoral Care.

September 28, 1969, was the last Sunday for the congregation to meet in North Scottdale. A Congregational Conversation is announced in the forenoon and a Fellowship Supper at 5:00 p.m. Attendance reported for September 21 is 63.

Although the records indicate that the closing was done after conversation and due processing, a church is not closed without pain. After 47 years some still remember the closing that way. As Nancy Sprinkle Keyser recalls, "Local residents that live near the North Scottdale building just quit going. It was very difficult to leave the church I grew up in." Jim Sprinkle says it was a "sad time."

Herbert Weaver grew up in Indiana and came to Scottdale as a young adult. As such, he could view the issue both ways. He recalls, "It seemed to me that the merger with Kingview would be a beneficial one. Some of the people went to Market Street, the majority came to Kingview, and some went back to their original churches."

I did not find a record of the disposal of the property. Rodney Cavanaugh remembered that he proposed donating the land to the local Native Americans. This was evidently not considered seriously by the merged congregation. ⇝

⟲ 4 ⟳

North Scottdale and Kingview United
Merger and Pastoral Relations

THE merger of the North Scottdale and Kingview congregations was accomplished without a resident pastor. As reported in the bulletins of both congregations, Edwin Alderfer took a leave of absence beginning on July 1, 1969.

Many details about the merger process seem to be missing, but there are scattered hints of what was happening. In the 1968 report of the Kingview Executive Committee, the congregational chairman, Paul Schrock, wrote, "It is obvious that a great deal of congregational energy will need to be expended during the coming year on bringing the North Scottdale–Kingview congregations together."

In 1969 the next chairman, Daniel Hertzler, noticed several matters needing attention: "We need to find a name for our congregation. . . . As soon as possible we must decide about pastoral services. The pastoral services committee will be expected to provide leadership on this question."

How the absence of a pastor was handled is indicated in the bulletin for January 4, 1970. It includes the name of David Hostetler, the overseer appointed by Allegheny Mennonite Conference, along with five congregational functionaries: (1) Director of Worship, (2) Director of Preaching, (3) Director of Pastoral Services, (4) Director of Education, and (5) Editor of Church Bulletins. This listing continued in the bulletins until July 12, 1970, when Edwin Alderfer had been called as pastor of the new congregation.

A copy of the 1969 charter membership of the merged group

has been found. There are 91 signatures, and eight of them continue as members of Scottdale Mennonite Church.

This merged congregation was to continue until 2003, a period of nearly 34 years. In order to organize the details, this era will be addressed in terms of the three subtopics: (1) Pastoral Leadership, (2) Congregational Life, and (3) Reflections.

SUPPLIED BY ALTA DEZORT

Barbara Paul, the first signer of the 1969 charter membership of the merged group

Pastoral Leadership

The separation of pastoral leadership from congregational life is obviously artificial. It is done to simplify the discussion to one topic at a time. The two were obviously interactive. Professional (paid) pastors were a new element coming into Mennonite church life in the latter half of the twentieth century. Kingview's experience illustrates some of the exigencies involved in this new practice. When the pastor is employed by the congregation, there can be subtle differences in the relationships between the pastor and the congregation. Between 1970 and 2003, Kingview employed one pastor, two pastoral couples, and two interim pastors. In addition there would be several intervals when no local pastor was present.

The length for a successful pastorate is a subject for discussion, but a longer pastorate is generally considered to be more successful

Helen and Edwin Alderfer, 1970–1983

than a shorter one. Edwin Alderfer became pastor of North Scottdale and Kingview in July 1958 and resigned from the united congregation on May 31, 1983. During this time he had a year's educational leave from 1969 to 1970, but was called back as pastor of the united congregation in 1970. So with or without the leave, he was pastor in this locale for 24 or 25 years. During this time two pastors came and went at the Scottdale Mennonite congregation, and a third was well into his nine-year term. It seems that the very longevity of his service puts Edwin Alderfer into the category of a successful pastorate.

Beginning in 1970 Edwin Alderfer was able to concentrate on one congregation instead of the two that had occupied his time from 1958 to 1969. In the 1974 congregational report, the section from the pastor indicates membership of 121, with 225 persons, including children, participating in the congregation. As in the pastoral reports found in connection with these two earlier congregations, Edwin had both positive and challenging observations about the congregation.

On the one hand he commended "the general cooperative spirit which prevails." On the other hand, "We seem to be somewhat divided, not in spirit, but in our manner of functioning in more or less isolated groups and individuals." Among the items on the report of the Executive Committee was number 9: "We received the report of the pastoral evaluation committee, [with] Paul Erb, Mary Hertzler, and Kermit Roth recommending continuation of our present pastoral arrangement." We learn from this report that a fifth of the pastor's time was being purchased by the Southmoreland Civic Association "to work with low and moderate income persons to assist them in securing safe and healthful housing."

This pastoral evaluation was based on Section 2 of the Kingview Constitution adopted November 25, 1973, where Article V, Section 2 specifies, "Pastoral-congregational relationships shall be the subject of annual conversation between the pastor and three persons appointed by the Executive Committee." Several more of these reports are found in the records; then sentiment apparently developed within the congregation that such an annual review was more often than necessary.

The pastor was interested in providing special nurture activities for members of the congregation. The bulletin for July 7, 1977, reports that "Edwin Alderfer will be participating in a laboratory training this week for leading a Family Cluster." On September 19 the bulletin announces, "The persons who by signing the sheet on the bulletin board in the late spring indicating their interest in participating in the Family Cluster have all been visited by Ed Alderfer: 15 children and 26 adults make up that group."

I believe that my wife, Mary, and I and our son Dan Mark participated in the Family Cluster sessions. I must confess that I remember very little, but I believe the purpose of the program was to enrich our life as a family, and it was typical of the sort of concern Edwin Alderfer brought to the ministry. The bulletin for December 3, 1978, announced another series of Family Cluster sessions to be held on Sunday evenings from January to March 1979.

Edwin wished to continue developing his skills in working with persons. On July 15, 1979, the bulletin announced "a congregational meeting at 12 noon to respond to the recommendations of the Executive Committee in relation to Ed Alderfer's request for permission to participate in a training program at the Pittsburgh

Pastoral Institute beginning this September." The July 22 bulletin reported that "at the congregational business meeting last Sunday, action was taken to adopt the Executive Committee proposal to grant a partial sabbatical. . . . This plan has been approved through May of next year."

The August 5 bulletin reported that "the elders have appointed a committee to be responsible for worship beginning in September." This was to relieve Ed Alderfer of some of his duties because of the part-time study leave taken during this year.

Bulletins at the end of 1979 point toward 1980 as a year for major expansion of the meetinghouse. A review of this process will be taken up in the next section of this chapter. However, expenses related to this expansion were to have an impact on relationships with the pastor. The minutes of a business meeting on November 20, 1980, declare, "Since the congregation prefers to have its resources in a church building rather than in a parsonage, it seems best if we sell the parsonage."

In the annual report for September 1981, the pastor's words are revealing. He reports a membership of 118 and also observes that "as Bob Johnson pointed out at the dedication service (9/6/81), the task before us is yet unfinished. It is all in preparing the old building to meet our educational needs. It is so for us in deepening our experience of unity, extending the involvement of more of the membership in the life and work and decision-making of the congregation, in increasing our vision for and practice of outreach." Later in the report he wrote, "Permit me to again express appreciation for the opportunity to have been in school this past year. I feel that the training is something I use every day in relating to and working with people in all aspects of my work, not just in counseling situations." He stated later, "I continue to count it a privilege to serve as your minister. Thank you for your support of me in my work and for the help you provide for my growth as a minister and as a person." This was after having begun as pastor of the two congregations in 1958 and returning from a 1969–70 leave in order to serve the united congregation (after North Scottdale joined Kingview).

However, in the same report the chair, Nelson Waybill, referred to the implications of the meetinghouse expansion, which is described in the next section of this chapter. He observed that "our building task as a congregation is not complete. Furnishing and decorating the new building is still to be done. We are now at the place for the remodeling committee to lead us in determining how the old building is to be used." He observed further that "in May 1983 our agreement with Ed as pastor will terminate. As a congregation we will need to make a decision with him about our continuing relationship."

The continuing construction to which Nelson referred would call for funds, and one proposed solution was the sale of the parsonage. As noted in an earlier chapter, the parsonage had been built for the Alderfers in 1958, and they had been charged rent by the congregation. Evidently by now the mortgage had been retired, and the parsonage was seen as a source of funds for use in continued work on the meetinghouse. This effort to obtain funds from the parsonage caused unfortunate complications with the Alderfers.

The issue is discussed in a 1981 exchange of letters between Nelson Waybill and Edwin Alderfer. Although the idea of selling the parsonage had been mentioned in the minutes of November 1980, the direct proposal seems to have startled the Alderfers. On November 14 Edwin wrote, "I feel that it is time for me to terminate my services with the congregation at the conclusion of the current agreement, . . . on May 13, 1983. . . . However, if that creates too great a hardship for the congregation, I am ready to terminate my services as of May 31, 1982, with the provision that we continue to live in the parsonage until that time." This was the closest I have found to a letter of resignation by Edwin Alderfer.

In response to these developments, the congregation appointed a "Pastoral Resignation Listening Committee." A minute from this committee dated January 15, 1982, states: "(3) The committee tried to assure the Alderfers that few if any people in the congregation seem to want a change as early as June. Second, if the people know that a change is coming, they can feel good about Ed as pastor."

It seems unfortunate that this financial situation was allowed to color relationships with the pastor. As it was to happen, in January 1984 the congregation received a gift of $141,669.98 from the estate of Zella S. Trout, an aunt of Ruth Sprinkle, a member of the congregation. On January 5, 1986, a congregational meeting approved selling the parsonage to Pastors Linford and Elaine Martin, and on April 13, 1986, the members considered what to do with the money.

Edwin did not cease functioning as pastor although reports of the Elders indicate the recognition of his plans to terminate on May 31, 1983. At the February 21, 1982, congregational meeting, "Ed briefly reviewed how he saw pastor-congregational relationships and stated that he had decided on the May 1983 date for the conclusion of his tenure as pastor. He pledged himself to faithfulness in his responsibilities and urged that we get on with our witness and work as a congregation. He led the group in working toward discovering what the Lord wants us to focus our attention on in the time remaining of our life together. As a sign of affirmation and commitment, Ed shook the hand of each person present.

On May 17, 1982, Paul Schrock as chair of the Elders asked Ed how he viewed his functioning in the congregation in the remaining year of his time as pastor. "Ed suggested three areas of focus: preaching, teaching, and visiting."

On December 1, 1982, Paul Schrock "reported the action of the congregation on Sunday morning to unanimously call Peter Dyck to serve as interim pastor for six months, beginning October 1983." But if Ed were to leave at the end of May, there would be four months without a resident pastor. "Ed was asked to prepare a list of pastoral responsibilities for which the Elders would need to make arrangements in that period.

The Elder's minutes of April 27, 1983, include the list: (1) Pastoral calling, (2) Pastoral work, (3) Overseer relationship and Conference Leadership Commission and other commissions, (4) Correspondence, (5) Membership records and files.

Also included is a list of church family members (updated April 1983) plus a list of persons baptized on April 3, 1983, and a list of baptisms, receptions, and withdrawals beginning in the 1960s.

Edwin Alderfer is remembered less as an effective preacher and more as a pastor whose strengths and interests were expressed through interpersonal relationships. His leave in 1969–70 was for study in this field, and when he ended his service at Kingview, it was to go for full-time study in this field. Yet when I reviewed sermon titles in the bulletins, I have found that he was addressing important issues. In the final year of his preaching at Kingview, he did a series of sermons from the book of Job. The bulletin for April 24, 1983, predicted that the title of the sermon for May 1 would be "Humor," but that bulletin is missing. His final sermon title on May 15 is "Blessed Are the Peacemakers." The bulletin for May 8 had announced "Saturday, 6:00 p.m.: Appreciation dinner for the Alderfers.

The May 22 bulletin reported that "Ed Alderfer conducted the funeral service for Homer Walters on Wednesday, May 18, at the Kapr Funeral Home." Some of us remember that Homer Walters had had an in-and-out relationship with the church and that he had been ambushed and shot to death. As far as I know, no one was ever charged with the murder.

On June 26 the bulletin announced, "Members will be asked this morning to respond to Ed and Helen Alderfer's request for their church letter. They wish to place their membership with the Pittsburgh Mennonite Church."

The May 13, 1984, bulletin reported that "Ed Alderfer received his master's degree in pastoral counseling from Duquesne University on May 5." Before long, Edwin and Helen moved to Goshen, Indiana, where he would pursue a career in counseling.

Whatever might be said about the relative success of Edwin Alderfer's 24-year pastoral service, I remember that he was my pastor for 24 years. I'm convinced that he cared about me.

Peter Dyck became interim pastor of Kingview Mennonite Church in October 1983. The October 9 bulletin has his name at the top. Peter's ministry was enhanced by his ability to tell stories based on his extended time in working with Mennonite Central

Peter Dyck (left), interim 1983–1985

Committee. On three Sunday evenings in January and February 1984, Peter told stories, beginning on January 15 with "Communists, Indians, and Grasshoppers."

A farewell for the Dycks was scheduled for March 25, 1984. But since the pastoral search had not yet found a pastor ready to begin, they agreed to stay longer. The March 25 bulletin includes a note from Peter and his wife, Elfrieda: "We thought this was our last Sunday here. The call to extend our service came very unexpectedly. We thank you for all your affirmation and encouragement. We will stay on a year, serving Kingview, but also give some time to the church at large."

The same bulletin announces, "Next weekend (March 30 to April 1) Linford and Elaine Martin, pastoral candidates, will be with our congregation." On April 22, 1984, the bulletin reported, "As a result of last Sunday's balloting and discussion, a letter to Linford and Elaine Martin this week gave them a unanimous call to be our pastoral leaders beginning [in] June 1985."

On May 27, 1984, the bulletin states, "As announced on Sun-

Linford and Elaine Martin, 1985–1996

day, May 13, Linford D. and Elaine Horner Martin have accepted a call of the congregation to become copastors of our congregation beginning June 1985."

Beginning on June 16, 1985, the bulletin lists Linford and Elaine Horner Martin as copastors, and on July 7 the bulletin includes a copy of their licensing service. The Congregational Response in this service reads in part, "The charge to you becomes a charge to all of us, for we are members one of another. . . . In common vocation with you as servants, we pledge to you our ungrudging support that you might freely exercise the ministries of leadership committed to you."

Linford's and Elaine's first sermons were taken from the First Letter of Peter, with "Hope" on June 23 and "Living Stones" on July 21. On August 18 Elaine's sermon title was "Time Out," with the text as John 6:1–35.

A survey done by the committee looking for the new pastors had found that preaching was a category considered most important by people responding to the survey. So it is of interest to see what kind of sermons the Martins were preaching in addition to the opening ones mentioned above. The June 7, 1987, bulletin announced that during the month of June the sermons would focus on current issues:

June 7—Abortion
June 14—Use of alcohol
June 21—Homosexuality
June 28—Sexual permissiveness

As we review the bulletins, we find that preaching was done by both of the copastors, though more often by Linford than Elaine. On June 5, 1988, the congregation approved the ordination of Linford and Elaine, which was scheduled for August 14 with the overseer, David Hostetler, in charge.

Linford remembers that when he was finishing seminary, he and Elaine were asked to consider copastoring, but after interviewing they preferred that Elaine have one more year of training. When the congregation thought it worth the wait and Peter Dyck took on another year, they were pleased to accept the call.

As evident in a congregational file on "Conflicts and Concerns" that addressed leadership and congregational growth goals, the assignment had its challenges, including questions that arose about pastoral responsibilities in addition to preaching. How much should be expected of a pastoral couple paid a single salary established by a churchwide agency? How would work expectations assigned to two people be balanced between them along with parenting and their personal lives? How often would a congregation not used to a woman preacher want her to preach?

Changes unfolding in a congregation finding its way through new patterns in copastoral leadership as well as fresh practices and opportunities caused challenges. This included the departure of one congregational couple. In the October 23, 1988, congregational bulletin, Lorne Peachey, congregational chair at the time, touched on "tensions and disagreements" in the congregation "particularly in relation to the tentative decision of one of our families to leave our fellowship" and said that there would be consultation with a conference minister "to help us process the current situation and find solutions where possible."

Among goals for the pastors was to develop clearer distinctions between congregational and personal responsibilities and for the congregation "to schedule a yearly renewal/revival commitment emphasis for focusing on individual spiritual development, the individual's relationship to the community of believers, and expression of the relationship through service and worship."

When shown the folder, Peachey commented on difficult days, on lessons to be learned as easing of relational strains was sought, and on the restored love between congregational brothers and sisters as God's grace enabled.

Linford also observes (in a December 3, 2018, e-mail conversation with Cascadia publisher Michael A. King) that many at Kingview Mennonite saw value in being on the cutting edge, were excited about trying the new copastorate model, and actually were prepared to ordain the Martins before they were ready to move forward. Amid many young couples in the congregation excited that Linford and Elaine were joining them in raising children, the Martins also felt the congregation's support when their two children were born.

Linford reports, "When we were hired a restriction was that Elaine was to preach only once a month because they were not used to having a woman preacher. I think that restriction was discarded within the first year. In fact they liked her preaching so much that when she asked to resign from her part of the pastoral ministry, one hope the congregation expressed was that she continue to preach occasionally."

Elaine would continue as copastor until 1991, when she resigned to focus more fully on caring for their children. Her name as copastor last appears in the bulletin for May 26, 1991. Linford was sole pastor until July 21, 1996. However, Elaine would continue to participate in the work of the congregation. A bulletin note for January 16, 1994, mentions her as a member of the research team for the LIFE process, a three-year congregational outreach program.

In the 1995 annual report, Linford indicates that he has been active in several areas: the congregation; Allegheny Mennonite Conference, where he was moderator; and the Scottdale Area Association of Churches, where he was a member of the Executive Committee and contact person for the emergency fund. He writes, "I participated in the Scottdale Ministerium, and I was a speaker at the Good Friday service."

In his annual report for 1996, Linford wrote, "It is difficult to know when is a good time to leave. Things are going so well. But after much prayer and consideration of when it would be better timing to move our family, we felt God leading in our decision to move." His report included the data on membership: "We received 26 new members: 14 by baptism, two by confession of faith, and 10 by transfer. We also had six who transferred their membership to other churches. Our total membership is presently 154."

A program in the file is "Farewell to the Martins. Linford, Elaine, Michael, Rebecca." Linford had served as copastor with Elaine from 1987 to 1991 and from then as sole pastor until 1996.

During the search for new leadership, Charles Shenk, a member of the congregation and owner of the local Brilhart Hardware Store, was called as interim pastor beginning October 1, 1996. The bulletin for October 6 reports, "With the approval of the congregation, Charles Shenk has been appointed half-time as interim pastor. . . . Charles will be responsible for preaching half the time. He will maintain office hours at the church on Thursday and Saturday between 9:00 a.m. and 4:00 p.m."

SUPPLIED BY AUDRA SHENK

Marian Shenk with her husband, Charles Shenk, interim 1996–1997

SUPPLIED BY CONRAD AND DONNA MAST

Conrad and Donna Mast, 1997–2003

On March 23, 1997, the bulletin reports that "Conrad and Donna Mast of Harrisonburg, Virginia, will be joining us for the weekend of April 4–6 as pastoral candidates." The April 27 bulletin reports that "the vote of the congregation to call Conrad and Donna Mast as our pastors was 97 percent, and they have accepted our call."

In the 1997 annual report Donna Mast wrote, "I never expected to be a pastor or to be married to a pastor or to return to Kingview. Yet here we are. I feel certain that God has indeed led us to live and work among you."

Conrad wrote, "We have landed and are running. You have blessed us in so many ways and made our move to Scottdale smooth. . . . I look forward to our journey together."

Conrad and Donna Mast served as copastors at Kingview for six years before the merger with the Scottdale congregation in 2003. Their comments in the annual reports are generally positive toward the congregation.

In 1998 they wrote, "Much has been learned and experienced in this past year. We anticipate continued growth and learning in our Christian walk together with the Kingview congregation. May Jesus Christ ever be Lord, and may God be praised."

In 1999 they report:

Church membership issues have been a part of our time here,
both congregationally and at the denominational level. In all
cases of church membership, we are reminded of how diverse
Kingview is. We believe that Christ invites all persons to follow him. That results in a wide variety of expressions and
worship. Faith and practice are crashing together in one um-
brella called church life.

In 2000 they say, "We [Conrad and Donna] are happy to have
renewed our covenant with Kingview and look forward to the next
four years. We anticipate God's guidance and grace sufficient to
meet whatever lies ahead."

In the months before the merger with Mennonite Church of
Scottdale, pastoral efforts would be related to the traumatic effect
on members of the congregation by downsizing at Mennonite Publishing House. In the 2002 annual report of the congregation, they
wrote of the

dramatic and tumultuous restructuring of the Mennonite
Publishing House. Our church community has been drasti-
cally impacted through job losses and relationship issues as a
result of decisions necessitated by financial issues. . . . This
has made our task as pastors immensely more stressful, with
additional counseling needs and processing emotional needs.

Fortunately our strength is in the Lord. We face monu-
mental hurdles and great risks, but the battle is the Lord's
and not ours. ❧

~ 5 ~

Kingview Congregational Life

THE annual business meeting report for September 15, 1974, totals 43 pages and contains reports from 22 individuals or groups, in addition to the report of the pastor (see the preceding chapter). These reports suggest a congregation concerned about its identity, nurture, and witness.

First is the report of Paul Schrock, chair of the Executive Committee. He reveals that the committee met quarterly and lists 14 of "the many decisions reached." Among these are the following: "(9) We received the report of the pastoral evaluation committee, Paul Erb, Mary Hertzler, and Kermit Roth, recommending continuation of our present pastoral arrangement." "(1) We agreed to recommend to the congregation that a study be made of our present facilities and possible need for expansion of our building." This concern would emerge from time to time and was developed into a major expansion of the building in 1979–81.

Charles Shenk, chair of the Elders, reported "a series of four Sunday night meetings to study Marlin Jeschke's book *Discipling the Brother*. Seventeen "understandings the congregation arrived at" are listed. Of interest is "(1) Church membership should mean something" and "(14) Discipline will never be an easy function for the church."

Daniel Hertzler, Director of Outreach, observed, "It is useful for our life as a congregation that we engage in a more or less perpetual study of who we are and what is our purpose. . . . The clearer we are about who we are and what we're trying to do, the better we are able to tell other people what kind of group we are and ask them to join for Jesus' sake."

Mervin Miller, superintendent of the Junior Department in the Sunday school, reported: "We entertained 25 invited older persons from the community at a senior dinner."

Marilyn Swartzentruber, Cradle Roll superintendent, wrote, "Seven enrolled and one added."

J. Lorne Peachey, MYF sponsor, said, "This past year has been a good one for the MYF. It was characterized by a lot of activity, a great deal of enthusiasm, and many good times together."

Roger Ledyard, congregational treasurer, projected a budget for the next year of $36,940.

There is a list of Sunday school perfect attenders, and the first session is announced of "Living Room Dialogues," an interdenominational program.

There is an announcement of coming spiritual life meetings with David Augsburger, a reminder that such extended meetings were a regular practice. In 1970 David's brother Fred had been the revivalist, and 19 persons responded. May 17, 1970, saw 18 young persons baptized, and one adult was received on confession of faith. Edwin Alderfer, who was on a study leave in North Carolina for the year, was brought back to take charge of this reception of new members. Of the 18 young persons baptized, Kim Miller still lives within commuting distance of Scottdale, although he attends Pittsburgh Mennonite Church. All the rest have scattered, although some are known to be members of other Mennonite congregations.

Bulletins provide a view of what the congregation considered important. In addition to the regular worship, Sunday school, and Sunday evening meetings, there were several annual meetings.

One was the yearly congregational campout, a weekend when all were invited to a campground. This had begun at Laurel Hill State Park in September 1970. The September 6 bulletin has an attachment with the program beginning on Friday evening, September 11, with a snack at 8:30 p.m. After facilities at the State Park were no longer available, this yearly event eventually moved to Camp Sunrise Mountain, near Markleysburg, Pennsylvania.

The congregation was aware of the traditional Mennonite practice, which expected women to cover their heads during public worship. On April 24, 1977, came a sermon titled "Veiling for Women: A Biblical and Historical Study," followed by a discussion session at 1:00 p.m. No record is available of a conclusion to this discussion. It can be observed that today most women in the Scottdale Mennonite Church do not cover their heads in worship.

The congregation celebrated its history. On May 1, 1977, there was a 25th anniversary and homecoming of the former Kingview congregation, with the address "What Is the Use of a History?" by Millard Lind, the first pastor of that congregation, followed by "I remember" recollections by anyone who wished to speak. On October 31, 1994, there was a 25th anniversary celebration of the merged congregation.

On October 5, 1978, an emphasis on the Christian and alcohol was planned for the Sunday morning worship services on October 8 and 15. A check on the bulletins for these dates documents this emphasis. October 8 offered the sermon "The Christian and Alcohol," and on October 15 a film was shown, "Chalk Talk," evidently related to the question of alcohol, possibly the abuse of it. At 1:00 p.m. there was to be a discussion "The Christian and Alcohol": "A panel of three persons will share their responses to the input on the sum of this and last Sunday morning. A general discussion will follow the panel." In the minutes of the November 16, 1978, Elders meeting, item 5 states, "It is reported that a member interpreted the result of the studies on alcohol and the Christian that for our congregation it is okay to drink. There were mixed responses on the part of the Elders as to how that interpretation was received." This, of course, serves as a reminder that spiritual life and behavior may be complex issues.

On October 8, 1979, is a report from the Elders on "extended Small Groups Discussion," exploring the "purpose of the congregation" and the "purpose of [small groups for] discipleship" and "to learn to know persons well." An 11-point description of the characteristics of small groups ends with this: "(11) We recognize the possibility of a person deciding not to participate, but the assigned leader and group would keep in touch and [have] spontaneous sharing."

Apparently the Elders hoped that everyone in the congregation would be willing to join a small group. Perhaps the construction project took so much attention in 1980–81 that the small groups were downplayed. The idea of everybody in a small group seems not to have developed. However, small groups did not go away. They are mentioned in records from 1987 and 1990. In Annual Reports from 1995 to 1998, J. Lorne Peachey is found as Small Groups Coordinator, and for 1998 we see 11 groups listed, with the names of persons in each group.

The twice-yearly observance of the Lord's Supper was taken very seriously in Mennonite congregations and included a preparation service before the event. Kingview followed this practice, but we find a gradual declining of preparation. On February 23, 1975, the bulletin announces a Preparatory Service on April 6, to be followed by Communion on April 27. In the fall, Preparatory Service would be on October 6 in family groups, with places of meeting listed on the bulletin board, and Communion to be held on October 19. On October 3, 1976, there is no mention of a Preparatory Meeting, and on April 22, 1977, the bulletin announces that all are welcome. So is a Lord's Supper to be a solemn occasion before which the faithful scrub their souls, or a celebration for all who confess faith in Jesus? It seems clear that Kingview moved from one interpretation to the other.

A special emphasis in May 1979 was on Family Week. A 19-page leaflet was compiled, including a detailed schedule organizing the congregation into seven Sunday evening groups "for potluck suppers, games, [and a] devotional." The plan suggested daily readings for each day from Monday through Saturday and half a dozen recipes. A less extensive program appears in the bulletin for May 4, 1980.

In 1980 it was decided to have an extended study of "Covenant." The theme proposed was "Kingview, a Covenant Community." It was found that the theme of the Uniform Sunday School Lessons for the fall quarter "would serve our congregation's interest in covenant very well." A seven-point outline is provided, ending with this assurance: "The accumulated findings of this quarter may serve as a resource for later work on a formal congregational covenant."

Summary statements appear in the bulletins, beginning with September 14. On September 21 was Summary Statement No. 2: "What is a congregational covenant? . . . We sense some anxiety among us on what a congregational covenant might really mean here at Kingview."

On December 7, 1980, Summary Statement No. 12 asked, "How can a covenant at Kingview be part of God's total plan for time and eternity?" It concluded, "Our covenant should help us live faithfully in the present, confident of our future in God."

The seventh and eighth graders had also written a covenant: "To be in covenant with God means God loves us, so we follow God. We believe in God. We worship God and do what God says. We trust him and believe that Christ saves us if we believe and accept him."

Whether or not a comprehensive statement on covenant was developed, the concern would continue into the new year. On January 18, 1981, Edwin Alderfer preached a sermon titled "Who Are the Mennonites?" A copy of the sermon happens to be in the file. He traced Anabaptist and Mennonite history, and at the end he declared,

> We are people of sincere and deep faith and of commitment.
> But we have not yet found what we at Kingview want to give
> ourselves to other than our life together on Sunday morning.
> . . .
>
> I sense an uneasiness among us about this. We believe
> Christ has something more for us. We seem to be waiting for
> it to happen.

I believe the Holy Spirit is saying to us, "Ask and it shall be given unto you, seek and ye shall find, knock and it shall be opened unto you."

I pledge to you my commitment to that task under the leadership of the Holy Spirit and through the study of the Scriptures.

Will you join me?

The biggest project undertaken by the congregation in the late 1970s and early 1980s was a major expansion of the meetinghouse. In December 16, 1976, a minute of the Executive Committee says, "Charles Shenk, as Director of Education, raised the question about the need for additional classroom space."

References to the facilities are found in bulletins throughout 1978 and 1979. A congregational meeting on January 7, 1979, elected a building committee, which "is (a) to bring to the congregation a facilities proposal for congregational action and (b) [is] authorized to engage the services of an architect, or spend up to $5,000 as necessary to develop the proposal."

Architects for the new construction would be Leroy Troyer and Associates, of South Bend, Indiana. A preliminary budget estimate dated May 23, 1979, came to $186,160, assuming "approximately $46,000 worth of volunteer labor and direct materials purchase savings." This would be a major undertaking, and members of the congregation made pledges toward the expense.

Maynard Brubacher and Mervin Swartzentruber were assigned by the congregation to be contractors for the construction. In October 2016 Mervin remembered that the cost of the construction was near the estimate. A report of the Finance Committee found in the files indicated $139,000 available. This suggests that the resources did not meet the anticipated cost. One suggested source of income was "Sale of the parsonage—appraised value of $58,000." In the preceding chapter, on leadership, we have noted that this proposal was traumatic for the Alderfers and that five years later, in 1984, the Kingview congregation received $141,669.98 from the

PAUL M. SCHROCK

Mervin Swartzentruber (above) and Maynard Brubacher (right), contractors

SUPPLIED BY MAYNARD BRUBACHER

estate of Zella S. Trout, Ruth Sprinkle's aunt. But in the meantime the congregation would be busy with the construction and the effort to finance the expansion.

A copy of the Troyer proposal is found in the records, along with proposed modifications by Mervin Swartzentruber. Both call for an addition of 4,350 square feet. Major features included an auditorium plus a large foyer, with a kitchen on one side and restrooms on the other. Above the foyer would be an open room with storage on both sides. The new facility would be adjoined to the older building by stairways to the main floor and to the basement. It was expected that the main floor of the old building would be adapted for Christian education classrooms. This construction would provide a major expansion of the space available for the congregation. It would provide a highly functional meetinghouse. This new part was wheelchair accessible, and just about anything the congregation wanted to do could now be done in the meetinghouse.

Plaque honoring Zella Trout, who gave the Kingview congregation $141,669.98

The church pews were brought over from the old building but not fastened down so they could be moved as desired. Eventually the pews were replaced by chairs, which were more easily rearranged. Flexibility was the key.

Willis Sommers from Ohio was employed as supervisor for the workers, and a trailer was placed on the grounds for him and his wife to live in. The trailer needed some rehabilitation, and Mervin remembers that he

> was just putting on the last piece of siding when the scaffolding broke. I fell to the ground with a broken heel. . . . They set up a plastic lounge near the church building where I could sit and study the blueprints and oversee construction. . . .
>
> I think it was kind of a blessing that I had to remain in my chair instead of actually being out to help with the construction. This gave me more time to study the blueprints and figure out details on ways to save money or improve the construction. . . .
>
> The church saved a lot of money by doing the work ourselves instead of turning the job over to outside contractors.

Construction of the addition to the Kingview building

> Also it was a great experience for members of the congrega-
> tion to work together, volunteering on this church work.

A 22-page list of volunteers and the hours they spent at work on
the project has been found. Someone must have counted the time
for the summary that appears in the paper. A clipping from the
September 3, 1981, issue of Scottdale's *Independent-Observer* reports
that Mervin himself volunteered 1,200 hours. His picture appears
in the clipping along with Stanley Yoder, "800 hours," and Mary
Hertzler, "400 hours." Maynard Brubacher remembers that he
probably donated 500 or 600 hours. An excerpt from the Connellsville *Daily Courier* for September 2, 1981, discloses "4,100 hours
spent by about 75 volunteers." The paper reports that "construction
began on the new addition in May 1980 and concluded this month.
. . . An open house will be held from 3:00 to 5:00 p.m. Saturday, so
that local people can view the church addition. At 3:30 p.m. Sunday
a dedication service will be held."

The annual report booklet for 1981 provides some evidence of
what the congregation was like as the major part of the building

DAVID HIEBERT

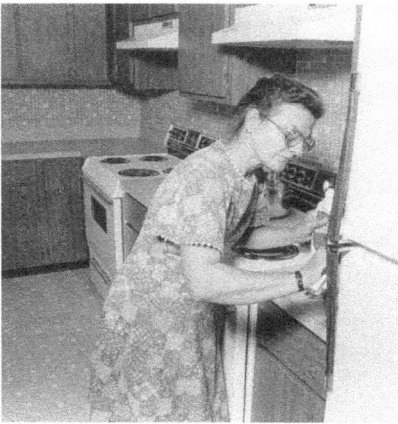

DAVID HIEBERT

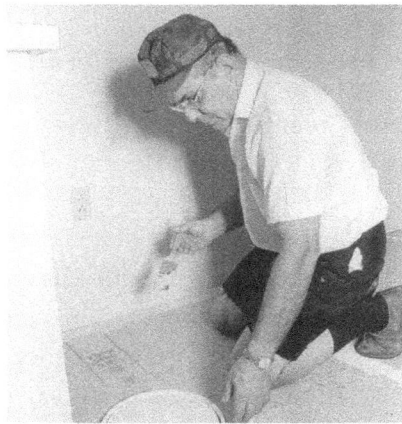

DAVID HIEBERT

Several of the volunteers working on the addition to the meetinghouse: top, Miff Paul, Neal Weaver; middle, Mary Hertzler, Stanley Yoder; bottom, Jan Brubacher, Ivan Moon

PHOTOS BY DAVID HIEBERT

The remodeled building with new entrance

project came to an end. The membership of the congregation is tallied as 118. Edwin Alderfer observed,

> As Bob Johnson pointed out to us at the dedication service (9/6/81), the task before us is yet unfinished. It is preparing the old building to meet our educational needs. It is so for us in deepening our experience of community, strengthening our experience of unity, extending the involvement of more of the membership in the life and work and decision-making of the congregation; and increasing our vision for and practice of outreach.

In the same report, Nelson Waybill, congregational chair, commented, "Although our facilities have expanded, our attendance has declined. What shall be our strategy for attracting new persons to Christ and our fellowship? That is our biggest challenge."

Two special emphases in 1982 were outreach and gifts discernment. Outreach was highlighted by Mervin and Arlene Miller, who attended a meeting of persons from the Hopewell Mennonite congregation in eastern Pennsylvania, a congregation that had grown dramatically. The Millers reported on this meeting and then began a Church Growth prayer meeting, which convened regularly on Wednesday evenings.

The gifts discernment process had begun with a list of nominees for the various positions in the congregation. This list was taken to the gifts discernment meeting to decide who should serve in which position. This procedure would be used instead of voting, and it was lengthy. A May 16, 1982, bulletin announcement said, "Our annual gifts discernment process begins this afternoon at two. We hope to conclude by 8:30." Obviously gifts discernment took considerably more time than simply voting.

On September 29, 1983, the new congregational chair, J. Lorne Peachey, read a paper to the congregational meeting titled "Working with the Stress Points at Kingview." He described five stress points that he had observed in the congregation: (1) Leadership: This was after Ed Alderfer had left at the end of May 1983, and Peter Dyck had not yet begun as interim pastor, although he would begin in a few weeks. Lorne observed that "one can't break 25 years of work and relationships and fellowship without it producing pain and stress." (2) New building: "When we talk about remodeling and about structure, not all of us are coming out at the same place." (3) Witness and outreach: "We're by no means agreed on how outreach should take place." (4) Congregational meetings: "Some of us attend each meeting faithfully. Others of us are fairly free on whether or not we attend those meetings." (5) Decision making: "How much should we expect all of us to be involved in most of the decisions we make at Kingview?

Lorne concluded with "Well, there you have them for what they're worth—five stress points I think we need to work at this coming year as a congregation."

A special program from 1985 to 1993 was the Christian Peace Elf, a reading program for children promoted by David Hiebert, the Peace and Service Representative. It provided a yearly list of "10 most wanted peace books," along with interactive exercises for each book, adult reviewers, and reports to the local newspapers. The intended audience for the program was 9-to-14-year-old students in the Connellsville and Scottdale area schools. A reader who completed the exercises for all ten books would receive a free book. According to the bulletin on August 3, 1986, the program had been well received. David remembers that by 1993 "we had great support from the adults in the community." But when we evaluated the program, "we observed that none of the 9-to-14-year-olds at Kingview or Mennonite Church of Scottdale participated as readers. [So] we quit."

In January 1987, Kingview began to cooperate with the Scottdale Mennonite congregation in sponsoring *Together*, a bimonthly newspaper, and distributing it to about 6,000 homes in the Scottdale area. "Its goal is to bring new people into our churches by showing that we are ordinary people who have faith."

In 1988–89 came the tension over leadership described in the section above. The congregation seems to have settled down after this conflict and pressed ahead with activities that seemed reasonable. Distinctive Kingview emphases appear from time to time.

On December 17, 1989, it is announced that "Kingview will be showing six videos of Active Parenting, beginning on Sunday evening, January 7. . . . There will be time for discussion following each video. Child care will be provided."

Recycling became an issue for the congregation and was done on the church grounds. On January 8, 1990, Alta Dezort was scheduled to make a "Recycling Presentation" during the morning service. The bulletin for that Sunday includes an insert titled "Recycling Information." It states, "The following items can be recycled and should be placed in the red recycling trailer in the church parking lot." Nine items are included on the list.

The Kingview and Mennonite Church of Scottdale MYF groups were combined, and the bulletins indicate an active program. On occasion fund-raising was done in a distinctive fashion. On May 20, 1990, the bulletin notes that on "Sunday between church and Sunday school, there will be an MYF labor auction. . . .

Alta Dezort, leader of the recycling program

Bids start at $20; payment is due at time of bidding." The funds were for costs to attend churchwide conventions.

The church published a pictorial directory in 1992. In the introduction Linford Martin wrote, "Thanks to Pam Philburn and Trellis Mellinger for giving leadership to this project. Thanks to those who contributed pictures and to Merrill Miller for laying out the activities page. And thanks to all of you for the time you took to make this album possible."

Two pages of pictures follow, which are labeled "Church Life," and then there are 55 individual and family groups, plus five photos of persons not available at the time the pictures were taken. One hundred sixty-nine persons appear in the photos. A family roster follows with members identified by a star. The starred persons number 126, not all of them resident members.

The congregation would give some attention to the question of Outreach. The bulletin for April 4, 1992, reports, "Last Sunday at our congregational meeting we voted to participate in the LIFE program (Living in Faithful Evangelism). This is a three-year congregational growth process, which enables congregations to be more active in sharing the good news of Christ. Roger Ledyard and Audra Shenk have agreed to be coordinators."

On January 16, 1994, the research team for the LIFE process reported: "(1) Kingview Mennonite Church has experienced a 31% increase in worship attendance in the last 10 years. (2) One response in the questionnaire would indicate that there is interest in outreach and growth, but it is not firmly rooted in our congregational life."

On April 28, 1996, the bulletin announced Growth Workshop 3 for May 19: "At this workshop we will celebrate what we have learned and accomplished in the LIFE process and will make plans for our church's outreach in the years ahead."

Beginning in spring 1996, the church published "Kingview Mennonite Church Newsletter," a four-page publication hand-delivered in the neighborhood. The church bulletin for March 17, 1996, reported that "this is a fulfillment of one of the goals from our Growth Workshop. The mission of the newsletter is to inform the community around us of who we are and what we are about." Beginning with the second issue, a subtitle is added: "Published especially for our neighbors."

The first issue is filled with news and comment about happenings at the church and includes an editorial, "What kind of church is Kingview Church?" The editorial has some history of the congregation along with "Kingview is a church that emphasizes peace" and "Kingview is a church that welcomes inquiries." The newsletter continued quarterly until the 2003 merger with the Scottdale congregation.

In 1999 the congregation was involved in activities related to the plans for joining of the Mennonite Church and the General Conference Mennonite Church to form Mennonite Church USA. The August 22, 1999, bulletin announced participation "in a denomination-wide study titled 'Envisioning a new Mennonite church.'"

In their 1999 Pastors' Report Conrad and Donna Mast wrote, "We thank you for the openness you have shown in ministering to one another and to us. Outside people have had a chance to see Kingview's mode of operating up close. Invariably we hear words of appreciation for what we are doing as a church."

In the year 2000, Olan Mills published a congregational photo album titled "What Is This Place?," using a title from hymn number 1 in *Hymnal: A Worship Book*. The cover of the booklet portrays the four towels given to the four persons baptized on March 19. One hundred thirty-seven persons appear in the formal photos, plus 24 more who were not available at the time those photos were taken.

Financial contributions to Kingview church reached a peak in the year 2000. The December 17 bulletin says, "Did you know that this is a year with 53 Sundays? The church budget is made out for a period of 52 Sundays. Executive Committee is recommending that all monies received as our offering for the last Sunday of the month be sent to others." On December 31 the year-to-date offerings as of the Sunday before were $1,402 above budget. A year later the December 30, 2001, bulletin reported YTD offerings $3,449 behind. The December 29, 2002, bulletin reports YTD offerings as of the week before as $8,661 behind budget.

The Kingview Sunday school did a special feature in the fall of 2002. One Sunday school class memorized the Gospel of Mark and presented it "in a coffeehouse setting" on December 8. The bulletin predicted that "each chapter will be presented from memory, along with dramatic vignettes which contribute to the stories."

Donna Mast wrote an article on this performance for the Mennonite press. The copy of a clipping found in the file was not identified, but it appears to be from *Mennonite Weekly Review*. She wrote, "The participants—ranging in age from 22 to 77 and from many walks of life—memorized and recited their portions of Mark, overcoming a general lack of stage experience." Donna quoted herself at the end of the article, saying, "The presentation started within me a desire to stand and clap at the end, yet there was something holding me back. It had been an awe-inspiring event, and I sensed a profound silence."

Other activities continued as illustrated by the 31-page Annual Report. But Jack Scott, the congregational chair, reported a weekend in April when Kingview and the Mennonite Church of Scottdale "involved Dale Stoltzfus to join us for a weekend to assist in developing vision statements for each congregation." The upshot of this was "to name a small committee to explore what would be the positive and negative results of merging the two congregations."

The November 3 bulletin announces, "Tonight is a special prayer meeting which begins a series of four Sunday evening prayer services throughout the month of November. These were planned in response to a call to pray for the congregations of King-view and Scottdale."

On December 8, 2002, came the word "The Executive Com-mittees of KMC and MCS are excited about the possibility of form-ing a new faith community in Scottdale. This vision has emerged over time in our work on vision statements, and the report of the Merge Exploration Committee, and with strong affirmation from our youth."

The March 16, 2003, bulletin states, "There will be a conversa-tion between MCS and KMC on March 23."

On March 25 came two reports: "The results of the merger vote were: MCS and KMC members each voted by 89% to approve the merger." "Four young persons are planning to be baptized on June 8. . . . These will be the first new members of the merged con-gregation." Attendance at Kingview on May 18 was 80.

The pastors, Conrad and Donna Mast, wrote "a pastoral note" that included their promise: "Our prayer is that the merged talents and energies of our two congregations will become a dynamic wit-ness to the community and the broader church."

The Kingview membership at the time was reported as 141.

Personal Reflection

I was a member of the Kingview Mennonite Church throughout this period. My wife, Mary, and I joined the former congregation in 1952, when we moved to Scottdale for me to work at Mennonite Publishing House. My lack of memory of details serves as an ex-ample of the importance of written records to preserve the history. I served in a wide variety of leadership roles but cannot remember anything I said and little of what I did unless it was recorded. I can report that I was the teacher of the class that memorized the book of Mark. I memorized the first chapter, and I can still almost recite it.

North Scottdale and Kingview began as Sunday schools when teaching the Bible was perceived to be a need in those communi-

ties. It was no doubt hoped that those being taught could be per-
suaded to join the Mennonite church, and so congregations were
organized with this in mind. It can be observed that some persons
joined, and others seemed to enjoy the teaching and fellowship without feeling a need for the commitment involved in membership.

Until the pastors began to be supported by the congregations,
they were closely tied to Mennonite Publishing House. This connection continued to be close enough so that when the publishing
house faced financial crisis and cutbacks, the congregations declined also (see the end of chapter 6 below).

Is there something to be learned from this church-building experience? As will be described in the final chapter, the Kingview
meetinghouse has become a childcare facility even though when it
was built it was probably the most functional and accessible meetinghouse in the Scottdale area. But a meetinghouse is only useful
if there is a congregation to fill it. 〜

❧ 6 ❧

Mennonite Church
of Scottdale
1960–2003

THIS is an effort to cover a 43-year history of the congregation in one chapter. The Mennonite Church of Scottdale (MCS) entered the 1960s with an interim pastor, but it was recently relieved of the responsibility to support the new congregations at Kingview and North Scottdale. In 1958 they had called Edwin Alderfer as pastor of those two congregations, which then appeared to be on their own.

The coming decades would provide opportunities for the Scottdale congregation to reflect on its own identity and develop new ministries. Since this was not a new congregation, there will be no list of charter members here. (Membership records are in the church's archives.) The bulletin for April 23, 1961, gives us an idea of the size of the worshiping body. It reports attendance during March. Sunday morning had a high of 151 and a low of 142. Sunday evening, 72 and 38, Wednesday evening, 45 and 32.

What shall be included when one is seeking to survey the 40-year life of a congregation in comparatively few words? One is inclined to take for granted the faithful efforts of those at work in the Sunday school, the Sunday evening meeting, the midweek meeting, the Women's Mission and Service Commission, and the MYF unless something unusual happens in one of these programs. More attention is generally paid to the comings and goings of pastors, insights and programs they have brought, historical celebrations, building construction, and a revised organization.

Sunday school superintendent Orie Cutrell challenged this as-

VIRGIL YODER

Mennonite Church of Scottdale

sumption in his 1961 report to the congregation: "As Sunday school superintendent I would like to challenge you, in this report, as to the importance of Sunday school and its possibilities. It is the church's agency for teaching the Bible. Sunday school is the church at work. We have a mission and a message."

I am proposing to consider the history of this congregation by decades, seeking to characterize each decade by what seems to stand out in that roughly ten-year period.

A Decade of Vigorous Activity: The 1960s

At the end of the first chapter of this account, I have noted that "on August 2, 1959, 'Urie Bender has consented to serve as acting pastor on a temporary basis during an interim when we will be without a pastor.'" Until May 1960 Urie continued in this role. From May 8, 1960, through September 3, 1961, the pastoral leadership as reported in the bulletins alternated between A. J. Metzler and Paul M. Lederach.

The March 5, 1961, bulletin announces that Gerald Studer has accepted a call to come to Scottdale as pastor. The vote for him was

Gerald Studer, 1961–1973

98 percent in favor. On September 5 the Studers moved into the parsonage. Then the September 10 bulletin records that Gerald C. Studer was being installed that day as pastor and gives the name of the congregation as Scottdale Mennonite Church instead of Mennonite Church of Scottdale.

What would eventually become a full-fledged ministry to deaf persons is anticipated in the bulletin for November 26, 1961, which reports, "The Deaf Community Bible Class was held on Saturday evening a week ago in the basement. Attendants, 15 deaf and 4 hearing. Offering, $16.15."

As with Kingview, the Scottdale congregation would be constrained to deal with traditional Mennonite perspectives regarding the practice of the Lord's Supper and issues of disciplined Christian living. It appears that the new pastor took leadership in these discerning activities.

On February 25, 1962, the bulletin announces, "Members and friends of this congregation: The congregational study meetings that you have seen announced will take up the following two fundamental questions: (1) What is the basis for church membership? (2) What is the basis for participation in the communion service? . . . Three midweek services are reserved for these studies."

Evidently the discussion of the Lord's Supper came to a relative consensus. On May 6, it was reported, "The recommendation to open communion distributed by letter last week was passed by an 89% vote."

Then followed the Conference on Faith and Practice, conducted by the pastor. The program on weekday evenings and on Sunday was as follows:

Monday: The Prayer Veiling
Tuesday: Participation in Secret Societies, Swearing of Oaths
Wednesday: Marriage and Divorce
Thursday: Litigation
Friday: Christian Love
Sunday Morning: Christian Baptism
Sunday Evening: Separated unto God

No concluding statement is found regarding these issues.

The question of a major addition to the 1939 meetinghouse surfaced from time to time. On February 5, 1963, the Board of Directors appointed a "Church Building Investigation Committee." On June 23 the bulletin reports that on the previous Wednesday evening it was "moved and unanimously passed that we move ahead with a building program." What was approved was not accomplished until 1966, and when it happened it was remodeling rather than new construction.

As pastor, Gerald Studer was particularly concerned to have the church engaged in prayer. In a document dated March 3, 1963, and labeled "From the Pastor's Heart," he says, "We all need the experience of praying together. One soul on fire kindles another." In consultation with the Elders, a plan was developed to arrange all of the members into neighborhood groups to meet for prayer in homes on Wednesday evenings. The March 31 bulletin includes a "Tentative Schedule of Meeting Places for Midweek Services," with everyone included. The bulletins for April 7, 14, 21, and for May 5 and 26 schedule these meetings.

Again on December 1, 1963, the whole congregation was organized into eight House Prayer Meetings. On December 8, the bulletin reports, "The prayer meeting attendance last Wednesday totaled 64 persons attending seven group meetings." Reports on these meetings would continue into 1964.

On October 10, 1965, the bulletin announces, "October 19, 12 noon—October 20, 12 noon, a 24-hour prayer vigil for the work of our congregation and the Christian Church in all the world."

As pastor, Gerald Studer seemed to wear well. On February 5, 1965, it was reported that "a surprise birthday party was held last Sunday evening for our Pastor following the evening service. He says, 'There is nothing special about turning 38, but there is something very special about turning 38 as the pastor of a congregation that loves you and goes out of its way to show that it does.'"

The congregation was encouraged to celebrate its history. During the Annual Business Meeting on July 22, 1964, "A portion of a letter from Sanford Shetler was read, calling our attention to the fact that this is the 175th anniversary of the coming of Mennonites to this area. He urged some public observance of this event."

Shetler's letter was taken seriously. On October 16 and 17, 1965, a weekend program was held along with a historical tour and special sermons in all three Scottdale Mennonite congregations. There was also a Sunday evening program featuring an address by historian J. C. Wenger, "Consolidation and Renewal, 1890–1965."

In addition, Gerald Studer edited a historical booklet titled *Over the Alleghenies*, covering various aspects of Mennonite history in this area. Although the celebration was to include all three Mennonite congregations, writers from the Scottdale church predominate, and it seems like a high point in the congregation's self-understanding. Included are chapters on the early Mennonite settlements in both Fayette and Westmoreland Counties, the story of whiskey making, how the town of Scottdale was developed on two Mennonite farms, and several chapters describing Mennonite perspectives and Mennonite relations with other denominations.

The chapter on whiskey making was written by Gerald Studer. It describes how Mennonites, like other farmers in this area, distilled whiskey for its economic value and portability to markets east of the Alleghenies; they also used it freely. But he says that Mennonites began to relate to the temperance movement, which began in the 1800s. He ends with a story told in the Stoner family of how Deacon Christian Stoner, who made whiskey, told his wife that they must either "increase the output of their still or go out of business altogether." She is reported to have said, "Christian, let's stop it altogether before we lose our sons. They are learning to like it too much." We do not know what the sons thought about it, but the story was preserved in the Stoner family.

Abraham Overholt developed West Overton village and made whiskey commercially. He was a trustee in the Alverton Mennonite congregation, but none of his children joined the Mennonites. In recent years West Overton has been maintained as a historical site. The current administrator is Jessica Kadie-Barclay, a member of the Scottdale Mennonite Church. It is reported that West Overton plans to begin distilling whiskey again.

Of particular interest in *Over the Alleghenies* is the chapter by D. Byron Yake on the origin of the Scottdale Mennonite Church. It recounts the erection of the meetinghouse in 1893 on land donated by Jacob S. Loucks. Yake describes how the congregation reached out to Kingview and North Scottdale and concludes: "The Scottdale Mennonite churches have a total membership of over 300 today. Many changes have been made and will continue to be made as the members strive to make their relationship to the church also relevant to the society in the twentieth century."

The ministry to deaf persons described above continued. On November 18, 1962, is the notice "The Deaf Sunday school Class will meet at 10:30 this morning. They will have a potluck dinner at noon." On January 20, 1963, "A picture is to be taken of the Deaf Committee after the service this morning. It is to be used in the *Christian Living* magazine."

The new construction that was anticipated in 1963 would be done in 1966, and it was extensive enough to suspend services in the meetinghouse for four months. On January 16 the bulletin announced that this would be "the final service held in our auditorium before the remodeling begins sometime this week." For the duration of the remodeling, the worship service was held at 4:30 p.m. on Sundays in the local Nazarene Church. Midweek services met in the Assembly Room at Mennonite Publishing House, across the street from the church.

On May 22, 1966, worship and Sunday school again met in the

remodeled facility. On June 19 the bulletin announces, "If all pledges are paid, we should have the project paid in full by December 31, 1966." Later records indicate that the fund drive did not end quite that well, but it was close enough to avoid being an ongoing burden.

Bible knowledge was considered important by this congregation. We remember the 1961 comments on behalf of Sunday school by superintendent Orie Cutrell. A special occasion on September 25, 1966, apparently initiated by Paul Lederach, Director of Education, was a "24-minute Test of Bible Knowledge" for the youth and adult Sunday school class members. Then on December 25, "A mimeographed report of the results of the Bible Knowledge Test given last September is ready for distribution today." I have not found a copy of this report.

Gerald Studer was active not only in the congregation but also in the local community and throughout the Mennonite Church. These activities are reported regularly in the bulletins and, it can be assumed, were within his agreement with the congregation:

> Pastor Studer is chaplain at Mount Pleasant Hospital this week. (September 15, 1968)
> Pastor Studer will be out of town all day Tuesday, visiting the American Bible Society in New York. (September 22, 1968)
> Pastor Studer leaves on Saturday for a four-day series of meetings at the Belmont Mennonite Church in Elkhart [Ind.]. (December 3, 1968)

Reports of MYF activity generally appear to be in line with what would be expected. However, one activity seems unusual. It is announced that on October 18–19, 1969, "the MYF is planning to meet an Amish church in Belleville. The group will spend Saturday night in Amish homes and attend the church service on Sunday."

Beginning in November 1968 the congregation joined with the other two Mennonite congregations in the study of Worldwide Hunger. On November 17 the bulletin lists "Questions and Exercises for the Study of Hunger Hurts. . . . (7) For those who can take it: Eat nothing but bread and carrot sticks between 12 noon and class time."

On November 2, 1969, the bulletin notes, "A poll will be taken soon concerning your preference for round notes or shaped notes in the new *Church Hymnal* to be released this coming August." I have not found the results of this poll.

A Decade of Change: The 1970s

Glenn Millslagle remembers that Gerald Studer once said a pastor should not stay longer than ten years. Records show that he stayed at Scottdale until July 1973, only weeks short of 11 years. But there was an indication as early as 1967 that he may have been getting restless. The Board of Directors meeting for October 10, 1967, discussed a leave of absence for Gerald. The idea was that he would exchange with a faculty member in one of the Mennonite seminaries. He would teach at the seminary, and the faculty member would be a visiting pastor at Scottdale. No final details appear about this possibility, and it seems not to have developed.

But pastoral change is predicted in the bulletin for July 30, 1972. It announces that "Sunday a.m. the Studers will share regarding the Lord's call to the Plains Mennonite Church at Lansdale, PA." The Studers would not leave for another year, so there was time for a Pastoral Selection Committee to work. On September 3, 1972, the committee was announced, and on April 26, 1973, at a special meeting of the Board of Directors, it was communicated that John Drescher would begin pastoral services on September 1 and deliver his first sermon on September 3.

So on July 22, 1973, the bulletin announces, "Sermon: Farewell Message by Gerald Studer." In less than six weeks his successor arrived. John Drescher had been editor of the *Gospel Herald* at Mennonite Publishing House. He resigned and moved across the street.

Drescher began strongly, yet records show that he resigned after less than five years. On September 23, 1973, the bulletin announces, "One Sunday evening a month Pastor Drescher is planning a period of praise . . . and a sermon. Sermons will make up a series entitled 'Basic Essentials of Salvation.'"

In the Annual Congregational Reports of October 1974, he states,

FROM *NOT BY MIGHT* (HERALD PRESS, 1983)

John Drescher, 1973–1978

As pastor, I've appreciated the sharing time and fellowship in the congregation. I sensed a warmth which is attractive to the outsider. . . . I believe our primary need is to reach beyond ourselves. . . . This year I've made 468 calls. The embarrassing thing is that I've not made a call on every family. . . . I feel led this coming year to spend more time with the young people.

On March 23, 1975, the bulletin reports, "Yesterday and today a group of 14 couples, with John and Betty, are in a retreat, which includes a full schedule centered on discussion of parent-child relationships."

In a November 18, 1975, report to the congregation, John shared his philosophy of leadership. "I believe in a leadership which seeks to enable members to be the church. . . . Leadership is not for the enrichment of the leader, but for the enrichment of those he serves. . . . Leadership is not real when people say, 'Look what our leader did,' but rather it is evident when people say, 'Look what we did together.'"

In the Annual Congregational Report for September 11, 1977, John wrote, "I'd like to share several ideas or concerns as I begin my fifth year as pastor, hoping that they may stimulate us to think together about how we go about helping each other best in our common task." His three ideas involved worship, mission, and leadership development.

On the first he proposed a new schedule for Sunday morning: (1) The Church in Proclamation of the Word, (2) The Church in Study of the Word, and (3) The Church in Celebration. He said, "I believe the key to our whole understanding of worship must center around the Word." Beginning on November 13, 1977, the bulletin follows this schedule.

A second concern was mission, on which he asked,

> Why is it that although Mennonites were among the first to settle in this area, we are the only church which has built a congregation by importation rather than from the community itself? . . . How long would the Mennonite Church exist in this area if Mennonites stopped moving into the area and we added persons [from the larger community] on the same rate as the past and the present?

As for Leadership Development, he declared, "We have, I feel, an abundance of persons who could serve in many congregations. We will need to plan specifically how we use the gifts of persons and develop such gifts."

In the spring of 1977, the Pastoral Committee had reviewed John's service and gave a positive report. The Dreschers' response appears in the bulletin in May 1977. "We appreciate the confidence of the congregation and feel led to continue and commit ourselves to another year of service. We deeply covet the prayers of each member and want to be more faithful in our prayer ministry for each one of you." As it happened, another year would see the end of John's service to the Scottdale congregation.

On February 5, 1978, the bulletin reports that at a Special Congregational Meeting, "Chairman [James] Horsch read Pastor John Drescher's letter asking for release from his duties here." The Pastoral Committee moved to release John and commented, "As a congregation we wish to express our gratitude to God for John's sensitive leadership, care, and love that was demonstrated throughout his 4½-year ministry among us." The committee recommended accepting John's resignation "effective May 28, 1978, with accrued vacation and benefits to extend until June 11, 1978."

A copy of John's resignation letter has been found. It is three short paragraphs dated January 12, 1978. He writes, "For some time I've had a growing sense that the time is here for me to resign as pastor." This "growing sense" had been expressed in a letter of May 17, 1977, where he wrote, "Four weeks ago I wrote out my resignation as pastor, asked to be released by the end of August."

The positive response he received to the Spring 1977 evaluation led him to reconsider, but by January 1978 he wrote, "We have now decided to ask for release by the end of May 1978." He added, "At present we have accepted no invitations elsewhere. I feel I need a year to sense where I am and what the future may hold."

Why did John Drescher resign as pastor after less than five years? There are reports that he was sometimes at odds with certain strong persons in the congregation. Rhoda Cressman remembers that he was inclined to scold the congregation for failures. One finds a hint of this in a repeated challenge at the head of the bulletin: "Have you interceded on behalf of this service?"

But the January 14, 1978, letter suggests that he may have been overly committed to activity outside the congregation. As with Gerald Studer, bulletins repeatedly report John's absence for ministry of various kinds and in other locations. The combination of congregational and deputational service may have become too much for himself and his family, and he decided he needed a break. In June 1980 the Board of Elders received a request for John's and Betty's membership letters to be sent to Zion Mennonite Church, between Harrisonburg and Broadway, Virginia.

Several other happenings in the 1970s need to be reported: The bulletin for September 13, 1970, lists seven young men away on I-W alternative service: Wayne Millslagle, maintenance work at Goshen College; Robert Bender, Mable's Trailer Park, Nappanee, Indiana; Tim Able, staff member at Mennonite Children's Home,

Kansas City, Kansas; Hesston Lauver, maintenance at an air-conditioning plant, Lititz, Pennsylvania; Ken Hartzler, in an operating room at Lancaster General Hospital; Dan Kauffman, Whitesburg, Kentucky. Two other developments stand out: (1) Major expansion of the physical plant and (2) the employment of Reuben Savanick as a pastor for deaf persons.

The congregation had had a parsonage for many years. When the Studers came in 1961, they moved into the parsonage, but at some point it was agreed that they should move out so the parsonage could be used for church activities, especially Christian education. It would be designated as the "Church Annex," and Item 5 in the January 9, 1961, minutes of the Church Board states, "The Christian Education Committee will be asked to make their recommendation on improvements needed in the former parsonage to make it more suitable for Sunday school use. The safety factor should also be considered."

This program came to an end in 1973. The April 15, 1973, minutes of the Board of Directors report, "The Annex was closed from public use by inspectors from the state. Reasons given were many. Examples given were [lack of] fireproof furnace room, fire escape, and electrical [requirements]." The Board perceived "five avenues to take." Of the five the church eventually chose the third: "Build an addition to the church."

A November 1973 memorandum from Joe Buzzard appoints a building committee. They are directed to determine the space needed, prepare plans for the new building, provide for removal of the Annex, "secure a builder to build the building, and follow through on the construction to completion." Minutes of the Building Committee begin on December 21, 1973, and conclude on April 3, 1975, when the building was essentially finished.

The architect was Samuel T. Redmine, who provided his service at $12 an hour. As reported on February 23, 1974, the proposed structure would be 36 × 49 feet, giving a total of 3,528 square feet, divided between "two levels, the upper one having seven classrooms of various sizes. . . . The first floor would be one large room with toilet facilities, kitchenette, and a free-standing fireplace." This appears to be essentially what was built, although the fireplace was not included.

It would be necessary to tear down the Annex. Glenn Millslagle remembers helping with this and that the lumber was used in other construction. Galen Sommers from Louisville, Ohio, was employed as director of the construction, and various members of the congregation provided free labor.

Relations with the architect were cordial. His charge for service was $5,124, and he then donated $900 to the congregation. (A March 31, 1975, Financial Report lists his contribution as $933). The estimated final cost of the building was $74,364.86.

The new construction met a need for classroom space. On January 12, 1975, the Christian Education Committee reported, "A tentative list of room assignments has been drawn up for the Sunday school in the new building. Room numbers are as they appear on the architect's drawings." The committee found rooms for nine classes with a tenth, the youth, in the basement.

Another development in the 1970s was a ministry for the deaf. The February 19, 1978, report of the Pastoral Committee observes, "The program of the Deaf Ministry is nearing a point where decisions need to be made regarding future direction and leadership." For the members meeting on September 17, 1978, the Deaf and Hearing Fellowship Committee reported that it "was able to meet a bit more regularly this year, with our main objective being the programs of the public meetings." The report ends with "We want to invite anyone to join us for our monthly meeting at 7:30 at the church."

The program for the deaf soon developed under more formal leadership. Paul and Ferne Savanick had given leadership for the program, with some financial support from the congregation. Their son, Reuben, was employed by the congregation half-time beginning in August 1979. The other half of his assignment was to be director of the Mennonite Board of Missions deaf ministries office.

On October 20, 1979, Reuben was licensed to the ministry by Allegheny Mennonite Conference. The bulletin reports, "The Deaf

*Paul and
Ferne
Savanick,
leaders of
a ministry
to deaf
persons*

and Hearing Fellowship began some 20 years ago as a result of a
concern by deaf individuals for a deaf ministry in this area. First
named the Deaf Community Bible Class, this group established itself under the leadership of Paul Savanick." In order to meet the
need for a teacher, Reuben Savanick was invited to serve as their
"pastor teacher."

   With John Drescher's resignation, the Pastoral Committee took
up the question of what kind of pastoral leadership the congregation would desire. The March 28, 1978, minutes of the committee
report the results of a survey: "The most favored model is a full-
time pastor who engages in teaching, preaching, pastoral care, and
is an enabler of gift development." So the committee began to contact potential candidates. Yet the idea of calling someone from
within the congregation persisted. The November 19, 1978, bulletin
reports, "The Pastoral Committee from time to time has received

the suggestion that serious consideration ought to be given to calling someone from within the congregation." So they invited suggestions for such persons, including the respondents themselves.

But the bulletin for February 18, 1979, reports that on February 11, "The congregation reaffirmed the desire for a single pastoral leader to be selected from outside the congregation." In the meantime James Horsch as congregational chair and David Alderfer as chair of the Elders would be compensated for part-time work on behalf of the congregation. Also the concern for preaching would not be neglected.

On October 14, 1979, the bulletin announces,

> Today begins a 10-week schedule whereby the preaching is directly related to the peace themes reflected in the Sunday school lessons. This series is planned jointly by the Commission on Worship, Education, and Service and the Board of Elders. It will include some special features—stories for the children, peace Scripture verses, choral readings, peacemaker registrations, and guest speakers Millard Lind and Jim Drescher.

Finally, on December 31, 1979, the bulletin reports the congregational action taken the previous Sunday: the vote "to call Robert Johnson as our pastoral leader was 102 'Yes' and 0 'no,' with two ballots signed but not marked."

A Time to Do Church "Right": The 1980s

From the beginning of this survey, Scottdale has been an earnest and hardworking congregation, but the record I have found for the 1980s seems to illustrate a peak in purposeful activity. In a September 23, 1979, report to the congregation, James E. Horsch, chair of the Pastoral Committee, observed, "I am quite aware of the frustration that all of us are feeling due to the lack of pastoral leadership. I sense that at times we find it difficult to maintain a common spirit." He observed that "compared to last year our attendance is down from an average of 141 to 121."

SUPPLIED BY JOE ALDERFER

SUPPLIED BY JAMES HORSCH

David Alderfer and James Horsch, interim leaders, 1978–1980

The search for a pastor would not be complete for another year, when Robert Johnson and his wife, Mary, were installed on September 7, 1980. In the meantime James Horsch and David Alderfer continued to be supported on a limited part-time basis for work important to the congregation.

One major change that came around this time was a new organizational pattern for the congregation. A copy of the Constitution has been found, dated 1976, with revisions in 1980 and 1981. An organizational chart shows a Pastoral Services Committee, a Congregational Chair, an Executive Committee, and a Council of Elders, with the Pastor and Church Office to the side. The work of the congregation is to be done by Commissions and Related Organizations. These are listed as follows: Education, Facilities and Finance, Fellowship and Worship, Missions and Service, Pastoral Care, Personnel, Youth Ministry, WMSC.

Everything done officially in the congregation would be related to one of the commissions. On January 30, 1980, John Spicher commented on behalf of this organization. He observed that the commissions will be (1) more autonomous and (2) responsible for their own budgets and (3) long-range planning. The chairs of the commissions would be named "Elders," and they would meet in a Council of Elders.

*Mary John-
son, with
with her
husband,
Robert
Johnson,
1980–1989*

From this historian's perspective, the organization appears a little too "neat," but it seems that people took it seriously. However, it can be observed that the work of a certain committee was sometimes found to belong to another committee. Of course, most of the volunteers were not being asked to accept a completely new assignment. The difference was how the activities fit together, with the advantages pointed out by John Spicher.

The entrance of the new pastor was accomplished smoothly. As the Johnsons pointed out on September 14, 1980, it was "the most meaningful induction service I have ever shared in. The reception we are receiving into your homes is thrilling. Certainly you are a beautiful family of God." As time passed, the Pastoral Committee conducted regular reviews of pastoral service, and all reviews were positive.

On September 13, 1981, Bob wrote,

Mary and I are continually grateful for the way the Lord has blessed us by bringing us to Scottdale. [Yet] learning to relate to a new congregational structure is taking more energy than I anticipated. . . . We are a hard-working congregation. . . . During this next year I would like us to give more time to being together just to experience friendship and love with one another.

A year later, in September 1982, he stated, "We are not as committed as we ought to be to 'drawing the net' as fishers of women and men. I pray that God will break me out of my feeling of comfort and give me a deeper sense of burden or concern for the 'lost.'"

In 1984 Bob reported that he had accepted two assignments outside of the congregation. Both of them called for more work than he had expected. It was, he said, "a year of almost frenetic activity [and] has in some respects been deeply satisfying, but also created within me a degree of frustration." The two outside assignments were president of the Scottdale Area Association of Churches and overseer on behalf of Allegheny Mennonite Conference for the Masontown and Pittsburgh Mennonite congregations. "I have been looking forward to this fall and winter. My prayer is that it will be a time when I can really refocus my energies in the service of the congregation."

At the time of the 1986 review and recommendation for another three-year term, the Johnsons indicated they would be interested in a career change by that time. The transition from one pastor to another was about as smooth as could be expected.

The bulletin for July 16, 1989, announces Bob and Mary's farewell, and on August 15–20 they moved to Souderton, Pennsylvania, where Bob joined the pastoral staff of the Souderton Mennonite Church. The July 2 bulletin announces that John and Michele Sharp and their family will move to Mumaw Street in the Thornwood section of Scottdale on July 25. On August 13, John preached the first of three sermons from the book of Ruth. On October 1, he was installed as pastor.

Another development of late 1979 and into the 1980s was the

SUPPLIED BY MARTY SAVANICK

Reuben Savanick, ordained as pastor to deaf persons, with his wife,
Marty, and sons Ben and Nathan

installation of Reuben Savanick as pastor for the deaf. His parents,
Paul and Ferne, had carried on this ministry for some years.
Reuben was a graduate of Goshen Biblical Seminary, and this
would be a way to provide professional support for the program.
Reuben's congregational ministry was to be half-time with the
other half time a program for the deaf sponsored by Mennonite
Board of Missions.

The half-time program with MBM would not last, yet the May
1981 Quarterly Congregational Report included the rationale for a
deaf ministry and a description of an "Endowment Fund," which
was evidently intended to support Reuben's ministry to the deaf.
On September 13, 1981, he wrote, "By being involved in a variety
of activities, hopefully I have been able to show through word and
deed the freedom and liberty new life in Christ brings."

Among the activities he reported were

to interpret special worship services [such as] Christmas Eve
Mass, as well as routine interpreting jobs ranging from legal to

medical to job-related situations. . . . In addition I was called to lead workshops, give speeches, and lecture on the field of deafness. . . . In January when the job became full-time, I began devoting a major block of time to Community Deaf Services (CDS). . . . In deaf ministry we are bringing liberty, new life, and peace through the breaking down of barriers.

But this financially supported program would not continue for many years. On November 15, 1981, Congregational Chairman James E. Horsch wrote, "In the congregation the area of deaf ministry is limited in terms of the members served, but the resources needed to meet their needs is large." So he refers to a "special endowment fund." It appears that this fund did not develop to the level needed.

The bulletin for June 20, 1982, announces that Reuben Savanick would take other employment, but "Reuben will continue to relate to the Deaf and Hearing Fellowship; he will continue interpreting for our worship service; he will continue to work toward the realization of a combined deaf ministry among several churches in our community."

So this unique program, a pastoral ministry for deaf people, ended after three years. It seems clear that the money ran out, and perhaps there was not a large-enough focused assignment to keep a young pastor occupied full-time. Yet it seems a notable effort: a modest-sized congregation providing a pastor whose whole assignment was a ministry to deaf people.

In addition to the regular weekly worship, fellowship, and educational activities, the congregation had special occasions to emphasize various concerns for spiritual development. For March 22, 1981, we read, "The Commission on Pastoral Care is calling the congregation to participate in a special service next Sunday evening at 7:00. The focus of the evening will be a discussion concerning the awakening of faith in the life of young people growing up in our congregation."

On March 22–24, 1985, there was a program called "Disciplines for Spiritual Growth." The resource team for this program was Gene and Mary Herr. "Mary Herr will meet with those who wish to search but can't commit themselves to specific disciplines as a lifestyle."

On December 22, 1985, Laurence Martin, Elder for the Commission on Education, wrote that the "Commission on Education is considering planning in-depth Bible study as a regular feature each winter." The first of these would be Romans 1–8, led by Paul M. Lederach from January 8 to March 5, 1986.

There was also a concern about evangelistic outreach. On September 5, 1982, the following question appeared in the bulletin:

> Do you feel that we as members of the Scottdale Mennonite Church should be doing more in our city in the way of evangelism?
>
> Are you willing to explore further how we as a congregation might reach out in our local community?
> —*Maynard W. Shetler*
> Sign here _____

I did not find a record of how many signed there, but in the congregational meeting for September 3, 1983, Miriam Beachy, chair of the Commission on Mission and Service, reported, "Early in the year we began planning for exchange visits with the rapidly growing Hopewell Mennonite Congregation. . . . According to the Commission's evaluation and the congregational response, the exchange was positive and will continue to influence us."

In January 1987 the congregation began to share with Kingview in the distribution of *Together*, a newspaper distributed to homes in the Scottdale area. "Its goal is to bring new people into our churches by showing that we are ordinary people who have faith. Our challenge is to share our faith."

On January 4, 1987, the bulletin once again names the congregation as Mennonite Church of Scottdale instead of Scottdale Mennonite Church.

Congregational self-criticism appears from time to time. On

September 13, 1981, Chairman James E. Horsch wrote, "Another agenda item is the gaps of age grouping in our congregation. The number of children is declining, and we are having difficulty planning a full Sunday school program." The Commission on Education added, "Adult Sunday school classes are not attracting some of our members."

A note in the November 8, 1984, minutes of the Council of Elders asks, "How shall we deal with issues? The issue of alcohol use in the congregation needs to be addressed in an intentional way in the future. . . . How do we disciple each other? What conduct is expected of Christians. . . . How do we confront one another in a redemptive way?"

Between 1980 and 1989 the Annual Reports show a decline of 18 percent in Sunday morning attendance from an average of 126 to 103. Some of this was apparently related to young people going away to school. In 1987, David Cooper, president of the MYF, wrote, "This year the MYF found itself with the smallest group in a long time. With only ten regular members, there was some trouble planning activities in order to have a big-enough group." However, in 1989 Steve Cavanaugh declared, "MYF was very interesting this year due to a very small group of participants."

As noted above, the pastoral transition from Robert Johnson to John Sharp was accomplished smoothly. However, on October 1 congregational Chair Arnold Cressman reflected on the problem of pastoral transition in the Anabaptist tradition. "Our Anabaptist theology may have a flaw that should be looked at. . . . In a more authoritarian system where the direction for leadership change comes from outside the congregation, the pastor may never become so fully a part of the congregational community, so it may be less hard to leave when the word comes."

Celebrations: The 1990s

John Sharp took up his preaching assignment with vigor. On January 7, 1990, the bulletin announces, "Sunday we will begin a series of

John E. Sharp, 1989–1995

sermons on 'What We Believe' between January 14 and February 25. What are our basic convictions? What does it mean to follow Jesus? How do we as Mennonites understand the Bible? . . . A sermon discussion class will be offered during this series."

Two congregational and community celebrations would be held in the 1990s, one in 1990, the 200th anniversary of the coming of Mennonites to this area; and the second in 1993, the 100th anniversary of the Scottdale Mennonite Church. The 1990s celebration emphasized geography. On March 25 it is announced that "the Heritage Bus Tours for June 9 and 10 are two different tours, Saturday in Westmoreland County and Sunday in Fayette County. If you drive around our community and wonder who built these many old houses, this tour is for you."

On June 10, 1990, the congregation held what the bulletin describes as a "Traditional Worship Service."

> This morning's worship service is our effort to recall the worship style of an earlier era. . . . As the congregation gathers, women and girls are invited to sit on the right side, men and boys on the left. The Sunday school "superintendent" is seated behind the pulpit. The song leader and any others who wish may be seated in the "Amen Corners." . . . Our congregation's tradition includes Sunday school before worship. We'll follow that format this morning.

After the Sunday school there was a "Sunday school closing," when "adults share highlights of the lesson" and "children quote memory verses."

The worship service included "Prayer [silent, while kneeling], a "German Hymn," and a sermon following the Scripture reading. The title of the sermon is not given, but it was to be followed by kneeling for prayer, concluded by the congregation joining in the Lord's Prayer.

Expected also would be testimony by other ministers present and also Children's Time, when "the congregation is invited to share memories of earlier worship services." Also, "after dismissal ushers will be waiting at the doors to receive your tithes and offerings."

Several nontraditional announcements in the bulletin include "Fellowship Time" with coffee servers and "6:30 p.m. MYF social evening and pizza at Don and Paula [Johnson's place]."

On June 7, 1992, the Scottdale and Kingview congregations dedicated a historical marker at the Alte Menist Cemetery near Pennsville. The ceremony included a picnic and remarks by various concerned persons. It concluded by "19th-century Mennonite singing," led by Jennifer Hiebert. The program brochure reports that "on April 23, 1991, the ownership and care of the property was transferred to the two local Mennonite congregations. The transfer of ownership will enable the trustees to open the cemetery again for use.

Monument at Alte Menist Cemetery

SUPPLIED BY FAITH ALDERFER

Burial plots will soon be made available to interested persons."

The 100th anniversary of the congregation was celebrated with a 30-page booklet titled *100 Years of Service 1893–1993*. It has 19 chapters and illustrations, which begin with Nancy Stauffer Loucks, 1808–1900, oldest charter member, and ends with George Loucks, operating a printing press at Mennonite Publishing House (established 1908).

The opening chapter by Pastor John E. Sharp is titled "Anabaptist Mennonite Roots of the Mennonite Church of Scottdale." It begins with a summary of Anabaptist history, leading soon to the Mennonite story here: "By the end of the 18th century, Mennonites from these Eastern counties [of Pennsylvania] were among the migrants who crossed the Allegheny Mountains in search of new land and economic opportunities." He summarizes the growth and decline of the local Mennonite community, observing that "this community's plunge into the industrial era, with its resulting wealth, also contributed to the decline."

Sharp goes on to write of the renewal, beginning with "a meeting which took place in the home of Jacob S. and Mary Saylor Loucks on July 22, 1893. Grandmother Nancy Stauffer Loucks (1808–1900) [widow of the minister Martin Loucks, 1798–1869] is given credit for fanning the spark into flame." He describes the organization of the congregation and the building of a meetinghouse along with charter members and other details, concluding that "with its membership, leadership, and organization in place, the congregation was ready to meet the challenges of the 20th century."

Other chapters cover ministerial leaders, cemeteries, women's ministries, music, youth, and children. Membership is plotted from 16 in 1893 to 166 in 1993. A rather odd chapter by Arnold Cressman, "The Denomination's Elder Brother," observes that in the past Scottdale had tried too hard to be an example for the Mennonite Church. Now, he said, "The Mennonite Church of Scottdale sees itself more like the younger brother—with sins to confess, with a journey to make back to the loving father whose arms are open."

The final chapter, "Common Beginning," is by J. Robert Ramer, then publisher at the Mennonite Publishing House, who writes that "Aaron Loucks, first publisher of MPH when it was established in 1908, was also a key ministerial leader of the congregation when it was formed in 1893. . . . Currently this partnership continues."

No one could imagine how this partnership would be tested within a decade. Indeed, I'm inclined to see 1993 as a high point, from which the congregation would gradually decline until the merger with Kingview in 2003. There would be two five-year pastorates between 1989 and 2001. Whereas the 1980 transition was a matter of weeks, it was more than a year after John Sharp left in May 1995 until Doug and Wanda Amstutz began in September 1996.

However, congregational activity and innovation continued. The congregation looked inward in an effort to provide biblical instruction and pastoral care. It also participated in the LIFE (Living in Faithful Evangelism) process in an effort to look outward. The rather novel organizational pattern with "commissions" remained throughout mid-decade and then was replaced by another novel organization with "ministries."

In 1991 Pastor John Sharp conducted a Winter Bible Study on 1 Peter. A year later a congregational retreat took the place of the Winter Bible Study. It was held at the Gilmary Retreat Center, near the Pittsburgh Airport. A February report on the retreat stated, "Our Gilmary Retreat January 24–26 was attended at least part of the time by 108 persons. The theme 'Gathered In' was developed in the worship and inter-generational sessions. With the singing, sermons, gym and Olympics, swimming, talent shows, meals, and free time—these all added up to a fun experience as a church family."

Winter Bible Studies and Congregational Retreats continued alternatively for some time.

The Sunday school was active. In addition to classes for children and youths, there were three adult classes, and they had names (from older to younger): Gemeinschaft, Hodotians, and Sojourners. These classes took turns managing the monthly fellowship meal.

It was perceived as particularly important to provide pastoral service—to make it readily available. On April 7, 1990, the bulletin announced, "Conversations on Pastoral Care," and stated that "Jim Horsch will be in the pastor's study after the worship service." This announcement appeared quite regularly, with a different member of the Pastoral Care Committee in the pastor's study after the morning service.

This program continued until November 2, 1997, when the bulletin announced, "There will no longer be a scheduled person from the Commission on Pastoral Care in the pastor's office during the Fellowship/Sunday school hour. . . . We invite anyone with a burden, member or guests, to come to us. Let us walk and pray with you."

In September 1992 MCS began with the LIFE (Living in Faithful Evangelism) process. One function of LIFE was the work of a research team. On January 30, 1994, the research group gave their report. Among their findings are these:

> (1) We are interested in church growth, but we are challenged when it comes to carry out biblically based evangelism.
> (2) We have not been keeping records of Sunday school and worship attendance, nor of numbers, names, and addresses of visitors. [As a researcher, I had noticed the absence of attendance records.] (3) We took in 10 new members in 1992 and five last year. Active resident membership is 113. Total membership, 161.

Beginning on March 13, 1994, attendance records again appear in the bulletins. In the 1990s these fluctuated above and below 100.

John Sharp resigned as pastor of MCS on May 31, 1995. In his resignation letter he wrote, "I have been offered an opportunity to serve as the new director of the Mennonite Church Historical Committee, based in Goshen, Indiana. I have decided to accept this new challenge. . . . To think of leaving this congregation and community tears at my (and our) heartstrings. This move is not motivated by any dissatisfaction."

*Wanda and
Doug Amstutz,
1996–2001*

JAMES HORSCH

The bulletin for May 21, 1995, announces, "Today, 5:30 p.m. Carry-in dinner and farewell for the Sharp family." That fellowship time ended by singing "Blest Be the Tie That Binds."

It was more than a year until the new pastors were installed. On September 29, 1996, the bulletin reports the installation of Doug and Wanda Amstutz, a young pastoral couple, he from Ohio and she from Ontario. On October 6, 1996, Congregational Chair Maynard Shetler wrote, "We are looking forward to new leadership with Pastors Doug and Wanda Amstutz. Renewed energy and renewed spirit are possible because the source of renewal is God."

In October 1997 he wrote, "The new pastors have been received well. They have made efforts to understand both old practices and the desires of the congregation."

At the same time, the pastors wrote, "We look forward with great anticipation to the coming year. We have done a lot of listening over the past year . . . [and are] learning where the church has been in the past and the direction we would like to see it go in the future."

The pastors were young people, and they were having a family. The twins Amani Debra and Abigail Anita were born on April 8, 1998, and Sophia Lorraine on October 10, 1999. These events somewhat complicated the nature of pastoral services, but reports indicate that the congregation accepted them with goodwill. One complication was that the congregation was ready to send the pastors on an Allegheny Mennonite Conference tour of Israel in February 1998, but the doctor said "No."

Another celebration was the publication of an illustrated congregational directory in 1998. It featured the current Mennonite slogan, "Vision: Healing and Hope," and the pastors wrote, "This pictorial directory is a symbol of our growing community at Mennonite Church of Scottdale. Together in our worship and service, we strive to be a community of grace, joy, and peace in response to God's great love for us."

Sixty-one family and individual pictures appear, arranged from A to Z, with three more photos of those who were not available at the time the photographer appeared. Seventy-six resident households are listed, plus 46 "nonresident and associate members." The tally indicates 99 local members, 31 nonresident members, and 10 associate members. Also, there were 21 local nonmember participants and some 50 children.

In June 1998 the pastors began preaching through the new Confession of Faith in a Mennonite Perspective (1995), with Sunday school classes discussing the presentations. On November 22, 1998, Doug and Wanda were ordained to the ministry. On October 31, 1999, Doug wrote, "Beginning in November I am challenging myself and Wanda to visit each one of your homes in the coming year as pastor."

Significant congregational activity included the Mennonite Youth Fellowship. For September 20, 1992, we read, "Don and Paula Johnson thank everyone for the celebration last Sunday marking the end of a six-year term as MYF sponsors."

In 1997 Deborah Scott, MYF president, wrote, "The MYF had a wonderfully full year. Much of it was spent preparing for Orlando, both financially and spiritually. . . . We also managed to have a good time, get to know each other better, and praise God."

On May 4, the bulletin reports that "20 youth are planning to attend Orlando '97."

On February 15, 1998, the bulletin announces, "Friday and Saturday the youth will be participating in the 30-hour Famine for World Hunger in Pittsburgh. Please pray for them as they fast for 30 hours and continue to raise funds for World Hunger."

In 1997 Ilse Reist reported that "WMSC experienced a very productive year. It brought together church members and friends to minister to global and local needs through a variety of projects."

John Sharp had written on October 7, 1990, "I have found the Commissions chosen to carry out the ministries of the congregation to be creative and resourceful. They have provided much useful counsel and assistance to my work as pastor. At the same time they have been receptive to new directions and possibilities." However, it appears that in the long run the organization by commissions, with each commission chaired by an "Elder," and a Council of Elders was not found satisfactory. So a new organizational structure was devised.

On March 3, 1999, the proposed new structure is outlined. There would be an Elders team along with the following ministry teams: worship, mission, education, gift discernment, and fellowship. There would also be a council and administrative team, with an executive committee, facilities committee, and the staff.

It appears that the ministry of the Elders was considered particularly significant. They seem to have picked up efforts of the earlier Pastoral Services Commission and gone even farther. On June 25, 2000, the bulletin predicts "a Commissioning Service for our Elders will take place on Sunday morning, July 16. They will be commissioned to assist in pastoral ministry of this church as Covenant Group leaders and assisting the pastors in pastoral care of the whole congregation."

On October 22, 2000, Doug Amstutz preached a sermon on "Why Covenant Groups?" The bulletin adds, "It is our hope as Elders, pastors, and members of our Covenant Groups that you will consider joining."

David Garber was one of these Elders, and he remembers that it was an effort to have all resident members and local attenders join one of these groups. They would have activities beyond the usual Sunday meetings of the congregation. He observes that this effort was not completely successful. An organized program in addition to the regular church services was more than some persons were ready for.

Yet the bulletin on December 2, 2001, was inviting people who might "like to be more connected here at MCS to join a Covenant Group." Evidently the program continued until the merger with Kingview in 2003.

Beginning of the End: The 2000s

What shall I write about this congregation when I know it will end on June 1, 2003, by merger with Kingview Mennonite Church? Shall I deal with it hastily, since I know the end is near? Not necessarily. The bulletins report current and predicted activities until the very end: birthdays, graduations, illnesses—happenings that are important to any Christian congregation.

The year 2000 seems usually active, with attendance above and below 100. It is announced that "the end of March it will be one year since we embarked on a new MCS organization." It is planned to have an evaluation of the new plan on March 16. On March 3 attendance is 103, and on March 24 it is 133.

On April 23, a Chat Room is announced for Thursday at 7:00 p.m. "All the women of MCS are invited to a time of conversation in the West Fellowship Hall."

For June 4 we read, "There are seven high school graduates from our congregation this year."

October 1 is announced as World Communion Sunday. "Please be in prayer for the service and for one another. . . . Am I in right relationship with God through Jesus Christ? . . . With fellow members? . . . With others beyond the congregation?"

"At 6:00 p.m. the Marriage Enrichment Series begins. This is open to all married couples from their 20s through their 80s. Pastors Wanda and Doug will host it."

On December 3, 2000, "Pastors Doug and Wanda invite all preschoolers through sixth grade to the annual cookie frost-off today at 4:00 p.m."

On January 7, 2001, "The Prayers of the Saints" column lists 14 categories from "The People of Colombia" to "Nathan Sprunger in the Marines."

The February 28 minutes of the Executive Team let us in on the future of the Amstutz pastors. They gave the committee a six-month notice of their plans to leave Scottdale at the end of August, 2001. Their purpose was to be closer to Wanda's family while the children were small.

On April 8 it is announced, "The Rev. Bill Detweiler will be leading spiritual renewal meetings."

However it is announced on March 25 that "this summer MCS and KMC will share our worship together over eight Sundays." Also on May 20th the song before the sermon is "Don't Be Afraid" and the sermon by Doug Amstutz is titled "Paralyzed from the Neck Up."

On May 27 we learn that "Pastors Doug and Wanda will be candidating at Grace Mennonite Church in St. Catharines, Ontario," and on June 17 that "Allegheny Conference requests prayer for MPH as they deal with many changes that are happening." Yet a slate is announced of candidates for congregational offices in the coming year.

The end of the Amstutz pastorate arrived on August 19, 2001, with a sermon titled "Pastoral Ponderings," by Doug and Wanda. It is followed by

Sending
Litany of Blessing
Circle of Prayer
Ritual Release
Attendance at the farewell service is 119.

On August 26, 2001, came a sermon by David Garber titled "Now What?" and a notice that "the Elders Team has asked David Garber to take requests for crisis care and co-opt the Elders themselves in providing needed pastoral services."

Now who would be an interim pastor? On October 21 the congregation voted by a 95 percent majority to call Charles Shenk as interim pastor. Charles was proprietor of Brilhart Hardware Store in Scottdale and a member of Kingview Mennonite Church. He was an ordained minister in Allegheny Mennonite Conference.

Sunday school enrollment numbers in the fall of 2002 are listed as children and junior youth, 18; youth, 8; adults, 54.

For December 8, 2002, we read,

Charles Shenk, interim, 2001–2003

"The Executive Committees of KMC and MCS are excited about the possibility of forming a new faith community at Scottdale. . . . Members will be voting on December 22." The recommendation to continue exploring merger with Kingview was approved by 87 percent at Scottdale and 94 percent at Kingview.

On May 18, 2003, both congregations approved the merger by an 89 percent majority. On the same date MCS held a fellowship meal for Charles and Marian Shenk in honor of his service as interim pastor.

Thus on June 1, 2003, the Mennonite Church of Scottdale, sometimes known as the Scottdale Mennonite Church or colloquially as the Market Street Church, ended after 110 years. Its future was to be found in the merger with Kingview Mennonite Church, a daughter congregation organized in 1952. This Kingview congregation was the result of a 1970 merger. The North Scottdale Mennonite Church had closed and merged with Kingview in 1970 because termites had invaded its meetinghouse.

The Closing of MPH and Its Effect on the Local Scene

The Mennonite Publishing House, founded in Scottdale in 1908 as the successor of several publishing projects among Mennonites, always struggled to be financially viable in a small denomination. Interested agencies and individuals were helping to subsidize certain publishing projects or loaned money to MPH as part of the mission of the church.[1]

"In 2002 after the restructuring of Mennonite Church, the General Conference Mennonite Church and the Conference of Mennonites in Canada into Mennonite Church USA and Mennonite Church Canada, the Mennonite Publishing House became the property of a new Mennonite Publishing Network with a board appointed by Mennonite Church USA and Mennonite Church Canada."[2] This new board and its executive looked askance on some of the loan patterns and accumulated debt at MPH. This led to dramatic changes. In addition, religious publishing in many settings was facing enormous challenges and changes.

Thus MPH declined in several stages. First came the downsizing. As employees were let go in stages, they scrambled to find other work. Some of the persons laid off at that time reflected on their experience.

The late Carol Garber, a member at Scottdale Mennonite Church, was a copy editor, and she said, "I'm angry and disillusioned." She reported that she began working at the MPH in 1990 and was excited about the job. But over time she became a confidential listener to people who were asked to do more than they could or who had made suggestions for improvement that were unwelcome to the management.

Jim Butti, also from Scottdale Mennonite, was foreman of design and composing. He was upset because his supervisory position was not acknowledged and he was dismissed in a block along with staff persons.

David Hiebert, from Kingview, editor of *Builder* magazine,

was told that his publication would be phased out, but he was invited to continue through the issue of May 2003 on a freelance basis. He commented on the difficulties of working freelance and also observed that *Builder* was one product that produced income for the MPH. David recalled his grief cycle:

> In the first days after getting the word of severance, I spoke lightheartedly about it. I mentioned it at the Rotary Lunch on Tuesday. I walked into Brilhart's [Hardware] and asked for the employment department. But then it hurt more. Why was this happening to me? *Builder* is a financially responsible publication. Why would it be stopped?
>
> Gradually I talked to more people, some from Kingview, some MPH employees, and others. Gradually it seemed that each time I talked about it, a little of the hurt would be healed.

Gwen Stamm, from Scottdale Mennonite, was a designer. She was dismissed because design was costing too much, and she was invited to continue on a freelance basis.

Jack Scott, from Kingview, was philosophical. He observed that each publishing house has its own team. He had been transferred from managing the bookstores to working in development and church relations. Ron Rempel, then the publisher, apparently found that he himself could do the things that Jack had been doing. Jack was too expensive. Jack reported that he had no ill will toward the organization. "I thought I had things to offer, but if I am to change, this is the time to do it."

Then in 2011 came the termination of the Scottdale operation by combining it with Mennonite broadcasting and moving the print-publishing work to Harrisonburg, Virginia. Three couples heavily involved in the Scottdale Mennonite congregation moved to the Harrisonburg area. They included Russ and Jane Eanes. After developing the business plan for the move, Russ moved from managing MPH to become manager of the combined institution, MennoMedia (MM). Also Merrill and Cindy Miller moved to Virginia so Merrill could continue his work in design with MM. Neal and Laurie Weaver likewise moved so Neal could continue his work with computers for MM.

Left behind were persons who either were not needed at Harrisonburg or were not able to move. They received severance pay for certain months and then were on their own.

Among them was Betty Dzambo, who lives across the street from the abandoned building and represents many community employees. She reflected on the closing and was distressed to remember how a program that had employed a hundred people when she began work there was reduced to seven when she was laid off. She said that the severance put her in a difficult financial position because she was not yet ready for Social Security.

She also feels that the closing was handled badly. "I don't think the decision was carefully thought through. To see them throw away books was painful, and to see the building sit empty is disheartening."[3]

In June 2017, Ervin R. Stutzman, who served in top leadership roles in Mennonite Church USA during the most difficult phases of the MPH downsizing, met with a group of those who had lost their jobs. More than 20 former employees attended the meeting, representing a total of 541 years of service. Stutzman invited them to share stories of the things they loved about working at MPH, as well as the pain they had experienced.

Employees recalled fond appreciation for a range of things, such as flexibility, the organization's family feel, and a sense of being part of a mission that reached beyond themselves. They also shared pain about the broken promise of supplemental health insurance, the brusque way many terminations were handled, and the unfair way the organization had been depicted in the church media. After listening to their stories of pain, Stutzman shared an apology on behalf of the denomination for a number of specific failures, and he said he believed some of the denomination's failings could have been avoided if he and others had chosen a different course of action. He also wrote a formal letter of apology, which was made available to the public as part of a news release in *The Mennonite.*

Finally, Stutzman thanked the former employees for their years of vital service to the church, and he pledged to find ways to tell the story of the publishing house's faithful work to a wider audience.

In summary, the closing of MPH had a heavy impact on the local Mennonite congregation and the surrounding community. Mennonites were no longer being drawn from other areas to Scottdale to work at MPH. Many non-Mennonite employees lost jobs. The closing had a flattening effect on local businesses and services. Yet the post office, built larger in 1934 because of MPH's shipping, still displays murals showing pioneer Mennonites at work. ⇝

Notes

1. John A. Hostetler, *God Uses Ink: The Heritage and Mission of the Mennonite Publishing House after Fifty Years* (Scottdale, PA: Herald Press, 1958).

2. From GAMEO: http://gameo.org/index.php?title=Mennonite_Publishing_House_(Scottdale,_Pennsylvania,_USA)&oldid=143312.

3. For other reports and analysis, see the following:

Rachel R. Basinger, "Merger Closes Mennonite Publishing House, Moves Operation to Virginia," *TribLive*, June 29, 2011, http://triblive.com/x/dailycourier/news/s_744413.html.

John E. Sharp, "A Century of Publishing Ends at Scottdale, Pa.," *The Mennonite*, June 1, 2011, https://themennonite.org/feature/end-era/.

Ervin Stutzman, "Letter of Apology to Former MPH Employees," https://themennonite.org/ervin-stutzmans-letter-apology-former-mph-employees/.

7

Beginning Again in 2003

KINGVIEW Mennonite Church and MCS merged on June 1, 2003, to become Scottdale Mennonite Church. A constitution and bylaws were written by Attorney James Lederach, and a minute from the Council meeting on December 7, 2004, declares, "We agree that the current church bylaws were adopted by the congregations at Scottdale and Kingview by May 18, 2003."

Leadership of the merged congregation was stable through December 31, 2015. Charles Shenk, the interim pastor at MCS, resigned on June 1, 2003, so Conrad and Donna Mast were brought along from KMC and installed as pastors at Scottdale Mennonite

VIRGIL YODER

Installation of Conrad and Donna Mast, 2003. Left, Charles Shenk; right, Kurt Horst, Allegheny Mennonite Conference Minister

MYFers Anna Mast, Hannah Miller, Theresa Peachey, and Jason Yoder, flanked by MYF sponsors Cindy and Merrill Miller, ready for the Bible quiz tournament at Carpenter Park Mennonite Church in 2003

Church. Allegheny Mennonite Conference Minister Kurt Horst was in charge of the installation and asked, "In commending Conrad and Donna for this ministry, will you also uphold them in it?" The people responded, "We will stand by them in their calling."

In January 2006 Michael Butti, a young member of the congregation, came to Donna Mast and announced his intention to join the Marines. Many in the congregation were stunned and uncertain how to respond. But it is reported that longtime church leader Peter Dyck spoke to him and said, "You have to follow your heart." Likely Peter was remembering that in World War II some 50 percent of American Mennonite draftees joined the military.

Eventually the bulletins began to call for prayer on Michael's behalf, and occasionally he would respond. On March 26, 2006, the bulletin announced, "Stop by the bulletin board and read a letter from Michael Butti. Remember him in your prayers." On July 20, 2008, he wrote, "Hello, church family, from Mike Butti. Please pray for my safety as well as for the family while I am gone."

After two tours of duty in Iraq, Michael returned and now works as a paramedic. He brings his children, Tranter James and Shayden Lo, to church.

In 2006 the congregation granted Conrad and Donna each a three-month sabbatical from April through June. Donna planned to focus on spiritual direction, and Conrad went hiking and attended a clergy-renewal conference. At the end they together visited congregations. In an August 30, 2006, response they wrote, "We enjoyed the freedom from anxiety that we found in our sabbatical time. . . . We hope to maintain that freedom by naming it and refusing to participate with those who would draw us into anxious feelings. Our hope is in God alone."

A congregational and pastoral review was done in 2007. According to the congregational meeting on December 9, 2007, "The returns were very positive for both the congregation and the pastors." A document titled "Results of 2000 Survey" provides summaries of "strengths" and "areas of growth" for Donna and Conrad. In summary, "You are both appreciated here for who you are and what you do."

Conrad and Donna continued as copastors until August 12, 2011, when Donna resigned to become conference minister for Allegheny Mennonite Conference. Conrad continued as sole pastor until December 31, 2015.

The congregation sponsored a ministerial intern during the summer of 2013, Jacob Landis, from Illinois, a graduate of Hesston College. The bulletin for May 26 announces, "This week we will welcome Jacob Landis as a Ministry Inquiry Program intern. For twelve weeks, Jacob will join us in observing what it means to be a pastor." After the summer Jacob continued his education at Eastern Mennonite University.

On Saturday evening, January 16, 2016, and Sunday, January 17, the congregation celebrated the ministry of Conrad and Donna Mast as they planned a move to northern Indiana, near grandchildren.

In the meantime the search began for continued pastoral ser-

David Mishler, interim, 2016–

Marcella Kohuth, secretary

vice. The bulletin for November 8, 2015, reports, "A motion was passed at last week's congregational meeting to begin the search for an interim pastor, with the preference for full-time pastoral service." On April 10, 2016, the bulletin reports that "David Mishler, aged 62, has agreed to be our new interim pastor, beginning in early July. Pastor Mishler will split his time during the [coming] 18-month term between SMC and Allegheny Conference."

During the time between January and July, the worship committee of the congregation was effective in planning the Sunday morning worship services. The Elders, hospitality, Sunday school, and women's activities continued as usual. There seemed to be no lost motion while the congregation waited for new pastoral leadership. Marcy Kohuth was welcomed as congregational secretary on March 18, 2011. Her continued work added to the stability of the interim period.

VIRGIL YODER

I-W men in the congregation: back, Jim Sprinkle, David Hiebert, Glenn Millslagle; front, Virgil Yoder, Rodney Cavanaugh, Herb Weaver

As a way for him to get acquainted, David Mishler asked each person in the congregation to provide him a 100-word account of "My Story." On August 14 he reported, "I have received 32 "My Story" submissions before today's deadline. Thank you so much for allowing me the privilege of entering your sacred space." By August 28 he had received 36 stories.

The merger of KMC and MCS left the congregation with two meetinghouses a mile and a half apart. We met in each building alternately in periods of three months and eventually of six months while the Council wrestled with the building problem. Both were reasonably functional buildings, although with its 1980–81 addition, Kingview was the more handicapped accessible, with worship and fellowship-related facilities on the same level.

Kingview, which had begun as a program to make Bible teaching available locally, now had few if any people walking to the service. Scottdale had members across and down the street, and others within several blocks.

In 2004 the Council proposed keeping both buildings, with the Kingview building to be known as "Scottdale Mennonite Church

Worship Center" and the Market Street building as "Scottdale Mennonite Church Administration and Program Center." An August 26, 2004, vote found only 58.5 percent of respondents in favor of the proposal, short of the needed two-thirds vote. So it did not pass, and the Council had to continue the search for a solution. On August 7, 2005, the bulletin reports, "The congregational vote of July 24, affirmed by 72% the Council's recommendation to move into the Market Street facility."

On October 23, 2005, the bulletin announces, "On Sunday evening October 30, the elders will lead our evening discussion to listen to the heart of our congregation. . . . Come and share what's on your heart. . . . We are calling this event 'Speaking of Loss.'" It appears certain that the loss to be discussed was the loss of the Kingview meetinghouse.

Dale Miller, the treasurer, reported that 2005 ended with approximately $1,200 surplus in the budget.

On May 26, 2006, Daniel Hertzler preached a sermon on the theme "Why I Wish We Didn't Have to Leave Kingview." Notes from that sermon do not seem to be available, but I'm sure I reviewed some history since my wife and I had been members of the congregation from 1952, the year it was organized as a congregation. I may also have commented on the convenience of its facilities.

It appears that the next Sunday was the final move to the Market Street facility. A bulletin note on May 28 calls for help "to be ready for worship at Market Street."

On October 1, 2006, there was a dedication service for the Scottdale building, recognizing 12 contractors who had been involved in construction work to improve the building. Also there would be a community open house: "Plan to invite your friends and neighbors for ice cream and fellowship so they can see our newly renovated facilities."

The building is not as handicapped accessible as Kingview. Outside ramps provide access to the main floor and to the basement. However, a lift (elevator) has been installed, providing access to all three levels.

An opportunity developed to dispose of the Kingview building. Lisa Bailey, proprietor of a day-care center called "Guardian Angels," showed interest, and the Council minutes on April 15, 2009, refer to negotiations and the details of a mortgage. The minutes of December 1, 2009, report the closing date as October 22, 2009.

Guardian Angels was not able to keep its part of the agreement. The January 3, 2012, Council minutes report that the deed has been returned to SMC control. There is some interest by another day-care center. On February 7, 2012, the Council minutes indicate that "Our Buddy's Place, a new day-care center which is leasing space from us, has opened as of February 6." As of this writing, Our Buddy's Place has not been able to purchase the building, so maintenance continues to be the responsibility of the Scottdale congregation. The facility is rented to them and has become, in essence, a ministry of the congregation. On October 27, 2013, the bulletin included an invitation from Our Buddy's Place for dinner and open house.

On September 7, 2003, the merged congregation accepted a covenant. This covenant is posted at the head of the steps into the basement. It reads as follows:

We are the community of faith named the Scottdale Mennonite Church. Together we will multiply our joys and divide our sorrows by sharing one another's lives. We will worship the Lord our God with heart, mind, soul, and strength. Together we will become better disciples of Jesus Christ, carrying his light and life into our world through the power of God's Spirit.

ART BY GWEN STAMM; PHOTO BY ROBERT EBY

The covenant is signed, and I tried to count the number of signatures. It is not an orderly display, but there seem to be something like 150 names. Attendance at the meeting on that day is not recorded, but attendance on September 14 is recorded as 126 and on September 21 as 107.

Sunday school classes continued. Bulletins in the fall of 2003 list four age-level classes for children and four subject-related classes for adults, declining to three for adults in December.

Congregational retreats for the merged congregation followed the occasional pattern of MCS rather than the yearly campout of KMC. The May 31, 2004, bulletin announces the congregational retreat for the next Sunday at White Sulphur Springs Retreat Center, south of Bedford, Pennsylvania. "This will be a weekend of dreaming, sharing, and laughter in a rustic setting of woods and streams."

On September 13–14, 2008, the congregation enjoyed a retreat at Antiochian Village Conference Center, north of Ligonier, Pennsylvania. The theme was "Speaking of Faith." Attendance at this retreat was reported as 53.

A retreat led by Lawrence Brenneman was held at Laurelville Mennonite Church Center on October 29–30, 2011. Three topics are reported: Missional Church 1, Missional Church 2, and Ambassadors for Christ.

On November 9–10, 2013, a retreat was held at Camp Sequanota, west of Ligonier, Pennsylvania. Regarding the retreat, a December 4 note of the Council minutes reports, "Feedback heard was positive for the meaningful casual fellowship enjoyed by many." About 70 people attended.

From September to November in 2005, the sermons during the morning worship were from the book of Revelation. During this time a Sunday school class prepared a dramatic presentation. On December 11, the bulletin announced, "Throughout the past fall an adult Sunday school class devoted itself to the memorization of the entire book of Revelation. The end has come, and they would like to share it tonight at 7 p.m."

The 12 Scriptures Project was advocated by Mennonite

Church USA. On April 28, 2013, the bulletin reports on it: "As elders we have decided to lead the congregation in a process that will help us identify and discuss Scriptures that have impacted our lives in the hope that the Bible Scriptures will become even more alive and present in our lives." The Scottdale Mennonite Church selected 12 Scriptures:

> *Psalm 23*, "The Lord is my shepherd."
> *Matthew 11:28–30*, "Come to me, all you who are weary
>   and burdened."
> *Luke 4:18–19*, "He has anointed me to proclaim the year
>   of the Lord's favor."
> *Luke 9:23–27*, "My disciples must deny themselves and take
>   up their cross daily."
> *John 3:16–17*, "For God so loved the world."
> *Colossians 3:12–17*, "Therefore as God's chosen people."
> *Matthew 22:37–39*, "You shall love the Lord your God."
> *Philippians 4:4–7*, "Rejoice in the Lord always."
> *Proverbs 3:5–6*, "Trust in the Lord with all your heart."
> *Matthew 5–7*, Sermon on the Mount.
> *Romans 12*, "Present your bodies as a living sacrifice."
> *Proverbs 9:10*, "The fear of the Lord is the beginning
>   of wisdom."

In 2014 the congregation supported Eagle Scout Aaron Coffman in his project to renew the miniature golf course at Laurelville Mennonite Church Center. A minute of the Council meeting on April 1, 2014, states, "We approved the project at Laurelville by Aaron Coffman, with the church and the members supporting the full cost of the material." Later his brother, Braden, created a gaga ball pit at Laurelville as an Eagle Scout project.

Sunday school and small groups continued but on a more limited basis than formerly. On August 2, 2016, the bulletin announced Sunday school classes for the coming year. "Kristen Savanick will teach the early childhood/preschoolers. Audra Shenk and Mark Peachey will teach the Middler class. Kim Coffman will sub for

PHOTOS SUPPLIED BY KIM COFFMAN

(Top) Aaron Coffman beginning his Eagle Scout project, with the finished miniature golf course (bottom left); Braden Coffman sitting on his creation of a gaga ball pit (bottom right)

them. Dirk Kaufman will teach the MYF class. Chris McMahon will teach the Bible study class."

I asked Chris McMahon to reflect on his class, which had first been mentioned on September 12, 2010. Chris is a "supportive attender," and his wife, Debra, is a member of the congregation. He began teaching, as he recalls, "when Russ Eanes left." (Russ moved to Harrisonburg, Virginia, after he was appointed as Director of MennoMedia, the merger of Mennonite Publishing House and Mennonite Broadcasts.)

Chris said,

> I cannot recall who asked me to teach. We talked about my limitations vis-à-vis the Mennonite tradition, so I offered to do watered-down versions of classes I taught at St. Vincent College [Latrobe, Pa.]. We have done classes on The Gospels, The Letters of Paul, A Survey of the Torah and the Prophets, Christology, The Trinity, and The Peaceable Kingdom. I have enjoyed teaching the classes, and occasionally I have used the feedback from my class in my professional writings. So it has been a symbiotic relationship. With Jack Scott, David Garber, Ilse Reist, Jane Rittenhouse, Gwen Stamm, and others, there is a lot of wisdom, knowledge, and experience that keeps the class on track and always in touch with the principles and history of the Mennonite tradition.

In the fall of 2016 Interim Pastor David Mishler led a class using *Undivided*, a church renewal book by Terri Churchill and Greg Boyd. David reported that about 30 people attended the class. He said, "I wanted to introduce them to Greg Boyd and have them do some internal worldview analysis since we need to change our thinking about how we view the world."

Small groups continued in the congregation. On May 3, 2017, I asked Jane Rittenhouse for a list, and she mentioned five groups plus the Comfort Zone and the Men's Prayer Breakfast.

In the spring of 2017, the Scottdale Mennonite Church seemed poised at the entry to a new chapter in its history. Interim Pastor David Mishler had been engaged as an agent for change. A Covenant Group had been appointed and was at work. The Council and the Elders had been on retreat in an effort to reflect and to look ahead. To get a picture of what is going on, in the next chapter I will consider details of church activity in the month following April 30, 2017. ⁓

8

A Month of Sundays

How can I end this historical account, which began in 1940? History never stops because life goes on. But the history writer needs to be granted a place to stop.

I have decided to close this account largely at the end of May 2017 by giving more than usual attention to congregational activities beginning on April 30. In addition I have asked several congregational leaders to write projections. But this is to be the end of the activities that I have been following.

I begin with the worship service on April 30. Congregational chair Dirk Kaufman preached from Luke 24:13–35, the account of the walk to Emmaus. The sermon title was "The Liminal Mennonite Church." He observed that "liminal space" is "between the now and the not yet. The liminal space is made up of the changes facing the churches." He urged that we "allow ourselves to step into the next space, . . . to reflect on where we are and where we are going."

During the Sharing Period, which followed the sermon, three Syrian women who had been supported by the congregation were called to the front for a sending prayer. The three were a grandmother, Kouhaïla El-Attrach; her daughter, Roudaina Al Chirity; and her granddaughter, Laya (Haya) Amer. Their American sponsorship had collapsed, so members of the congregation moved in to help. Particularly active were Arlene Miller, David Garber, and members of the Comfort Zone. Now the three were planning to return to Lebanon or Syria. The closing hymn was "Blest Be the Tie That Binds."

SUSAN ANSELL

SARAH ALLEGRA

(Left) Dave Garber and Kouhaïla El-Attrach; (right) Arlene Miller with Roudaina Al Chirity and her daughter, Laya (Haya) Amer

Fifteen persons are listed as having some responsibility during the worship service, the fellowship time, or the Sunday school. The offering was $1,711.24 in comparison with $2,116 needed. In addition was the Mutual Aid offering, which totaled $950. Attendance was 64.

On Thursday, May 4, the Comfort Zone convened for their regular monthly meeting, which included knotting comforters, a program, and a noonday meal. That day's program was a conversation with Roudaina about her life and her plans to move to Lebanon or Syria, her native country. Ilse Reist explained the source of the term "Comfort Zone." She said that Rita Yoder had shown impatience with the label "Mennonite Women," and so it was replaced by Comfort Zone.

Ilse pointed out that the word *comfort* is interpreted broadly: not only comforters for those needing them, but also comfort for

Comfort Zone leaders: Rita Yoder, Sandra Johnson, Ilse Reist, Joyce Millslagle, Arlene Miller

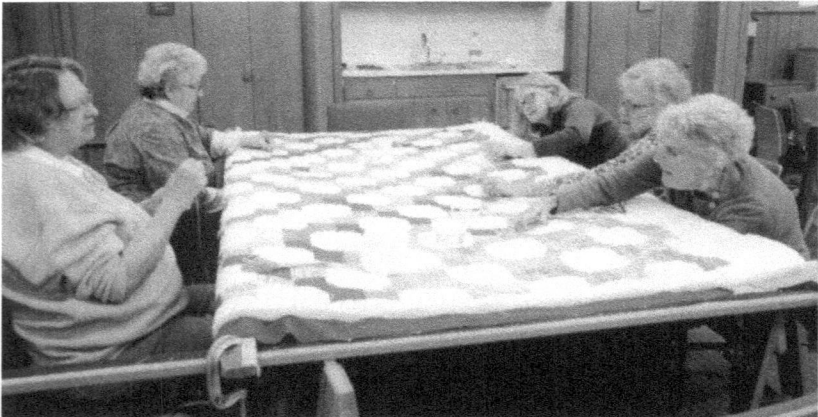

Knotting a comforter at Comfort Zone: Sandra Stambaugh, Jane Sprinkle, Becky King, Phebe Cressman, Arlene Miller

one another and for others in need of encouragement. One of the comforters was given to a local family who lost their home in a fire. Most are sent to Mennonite Central Committee. The comfort of the luncheon at noon was extended to husbands and others, including this writer and his wife, Mary, who had worked for the Comfort Zone as long as she was able.

VIRGIL YODER

*(Above) Atten-
dees at the Men's
Prayer Breakfast
in November
2014; (left)
J. T. Runyon,
Mark Peachey,
Daniel Lint,
April 14, 2018*

In the flurry of arranging to cover the work of the congregation during the month of May, 2017, one activity was overlooked: Men's Prayer Breakfast coordinated by Daniel Lint, which meets the second Saturday from September through May. In order to have this included, the breakfast for April 14, 2018, is reported here.

Pancakes and sausage were served by J. T. Runyon, and the meditation was led by Mark Peachey. He read the Beatitudes from Matthew 5 and asked, "What does it mean to be faithful to God? How do we live our lives knowing we are going to die?"

Herbert Weaver commented that "I think about it daily. My oldest brother is 98. He has cancer and is given six to nine months to live. But I have concluded that dying isn't the worst thing that can happen to you." The group of men, mostly 70 or older, seemed to agree. Mark's conclusion was hopeful: "The fact that we are going to die need not deprive us of the joy of living."

VIRGIL YODER

Dorothy and Tony Ramos, who began Fresh Express in 2000

VIRGIL YODER

Gerald and Nina Buzzard, directors, 2006–

On May 7 Interim Pastor David Mishler preached the first of a projected series of six sermons on the theme of "Sabbath." After a reading of the Ten Commandments, he pointed out that the first commandment "No other gods" was basic then and is basic now. Prevailing gods today include (1) consumerism, (2) opportunities, (3) entertainment, (4) violence. All of these produce anxiety, but the Sabbath provides an alternative, an alternative emphasized by Jesus in Matthew 6, where he stresses the futility of trying to serve two masters. David asked us to focus on the Sabbath as a way of life more than just as a special day.

Attendance on May 7 was 50. The offering was $921 plus $50 for Mutual Aid.

On Wednesday, May 10, came Fresh Express, a food distribution service begun by Tony and Dorothy Ramos in the year 2000 and now continued by the congregation. The food comes from the Westmoreland County Food Bank three times a year, and the cost of delivery is paid by the congregation.

VIRGIL YODER

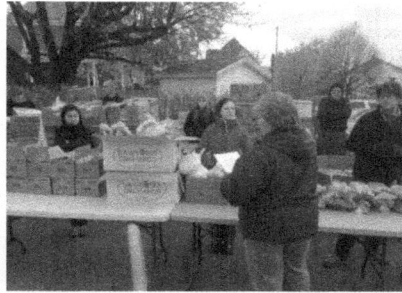

Fresh Express volunteers

VIRGIL YODER

The food was unloaded from the Food Bank trucks, and tables were set up in the alley behind the church building. Representatives from the Food Bank directed the distribution. However, in the church basement Nina and Gerald Buzzard registered the recipients, assisted by Jim and Jane Sprinkle and Jim Butti. After they had received their tickets, people were welcomed by Audra Shenk (chair of the Missions and Service Committee) for coffee or tea and food samples—food recommended as healthy.

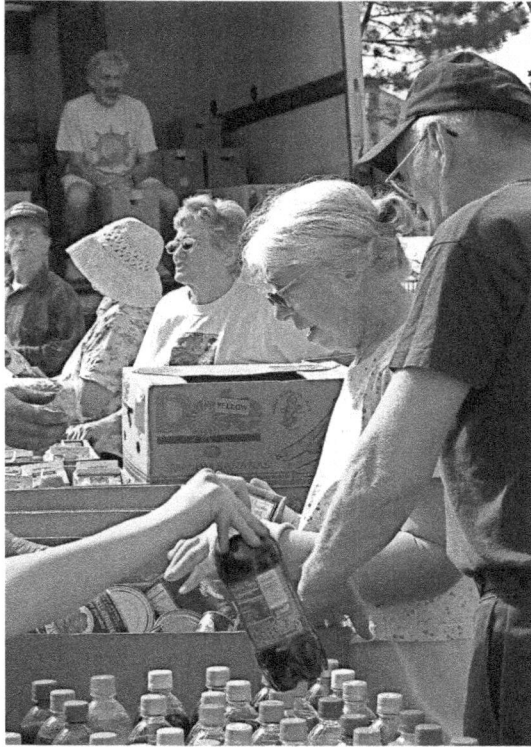

The food distribution was done by volunteers behind the tables: members of the Scottdale congregation, friends, and on this day the German Club from the Connellsville Area High School. Food was provided for 85 to 90 households.

David Mishler's sermon title for May 14 was "Sabbath: From Anxiety to Thanksgiving," with the text from Deuteronomy 5:1–22. He said that whereas Exodus 20:1–17 emphasizes the Lord as the Creator and that Sabbath establishes the rhythm of the week, Deuteronomy was written for the next generation, and they are not to forget the slavery in Egypt. Added to the list of those who are to rest are slaves and resident aliens, "so they may rest as you do."

Following worship there was a "Town Hall Meeting." A hand-out clarified the "Purpose: To offer a forum to introduce and discuss immediate and long-term vision for our congregation." Among the questions raised was "If it were more important to be sent to be with our neighbors rather than to attract them to our worship, what would our Christianity look like?"

Among the wide-ranging group of observations were these: (1) For some people Mennonites are unpopular because of our peace position. (2) Some have seen us as unwilling to participate in community-wide events, although our practice has become more open. Jack Scott observed that we should not lose our image of who we are. In our effort to be everything to everybody, we

Children's time led by Kim Coffman on May 6, 2018

AUDRA SHENK

VIRGIL YODER

Worship service at Scottdale Mennonite Church during Advent 2006

should not forget what it means to be Anabaptist.

Jim Butti said that we have lost the ability to have fun together.

Dirk Kaufman pointed out that we were in a process along with Allegheny Mennonite Conference and Mennonite Church USA.

Shelby Echard was concerned about people who have stopped attending. Evidently no one felt called to contact them. This is a reminder that in the old days Sunday school classes kept attendance records. When someone was missing, it was simple to notice that.

Attendance on May 14 was 52. The offering was $1,171 plus $50 for Mutual Aid.

On May 21 the first hymn was number 32 in *Hymnal: A Worship Book*, "Our Father God, Thy Name We Praise," written by the Dutch Mennonite Leenaert Clock in the seventeenth century. This is a hymn that the Old Order Amish sing in German at every worship service, using the traditional music that appears as number 33 in *HWB*.

During Children's Time, Kim Coffman urged children to consider important choices. She had help from the devil, a young man in black, and a Christian, a young woman in white. The choice was represented as a rag on a rope, moved back and forth until, with the quotation of James 4:7, the devil was made to "flee."

David Mishler preached the third of his series on Sabbath, with a text from Isaiah 56:1–8. This, he said, is a new teaching about Sabbath in a new time. The writing period is after the exile, and the emphasis is on inclusion rather than exclusion. Specifically to be included are foreigners and eunuchs, outsiders and the sexually impaired. Both are welcomed if they will keep the Sabbath. This is in direct opposition to Deuteronomy 23:1–6, which excludes from worship anyone whose "testicles are crushed" as well as "Ammonites and Moabites," because of their lack of hospitality to Israel during the exodus from Egypt.

In this new time the prophet is free to contradict the confession of faith in Deuteronomy 23. However, as Pastor David pointed out, ethnic purity was never really the case for the Israelites. Exodus 12:37–38 reports that "a mixed crowd also went with them" in the escape from Egypt. But evidently the temptation for exclusion would always be present. He said, "Isaiah speaks to a new generation, more mixed up. There was need for a new purpose for Sabbath." The opening line in Isaiah 56 is "Maintain justice and do what is right." That is more important than ethnic purity.

"God's message is always adapted to real history. Each generation is asked to respond to a new situation." This was the third of a projected six sermons on the theme of Sabbath.

Attendance on May 21 was 58. The offering was $1,204.22 of a needed $2,116. Also there was $75 for Mutual Aid.

The preacher on May 29 was Wes Bergen, pastor of the Morgantown, West Virginia, Church of the Brethren. His theme was "Ascending to Heaven While Rooted on the Earth." He used four New Testament texts: from John 17, 1 Peter 4, 1 Peter 5, and Acts 1.

His point was that eternal life as described by Jesus in John 17 is not just far away in the future but is available now. Eternal life is to know God and Jesus Christ. If we know God, we must be important people. But not so fast since 1 Peter points out that Christians should expect persecution, yet in Acts 1 Jesus' disciples were expecting to rule. But they should not wish to rule. Rather, they

Banner made up of purples, blues, and gold, brush-lettered by Gwen Stamm, on fabrics sewn together by Audra Shenk

are to be witnesses. That is our calling today: not to rule but to be witnesses. The worship ended by singing the hymn "When Peace Like a River."

Attendance was 58 and the offering $3,358.

I asked several leaders to project goals for the Scottdale congregation in the near future. And I have a closing comment.

Because there would be no Sunday school for the summer, Audra Shenk would be leading Children's Church. She said,

All children will meet together for the summer months. The material used will be "Shine: Living in God's Light."

She observed further,

As the size of our congregation shrinks, we will need to find new ways to build Sunday school for the varying ages of the few children who attend.

David Mishler responded as follows:

CHRIS MOSEMANN

As interim pastor, my primary goal for the Scottdale congregation is to make a candid and accurate assessment of "where we are" so we can begin to better ask, "Where do we want to go from here?" I see my role as holding up a mirror to help us see clearly what is often overlooked because it becomes a part of the fabric, and we don't see or name what is in front of us. A second role is to place our current context into the larger worldview of our culture and current Christian witness.

My sermons for the past year have mostly been "worldview" sermons. I believe we have been greatly influenced by and have become acculturated toward the American dream and have become much less counterculture in our mind-sets. The current Sabbath series is an attempt to reenvision what it means to work in the way of Jesus, resisting our tendencies toward acculturation (Brueggemann). As an interim pastor and conference minister, my task is eventually to help articulate a vision and identify with the congregation so that a

long-term pastor can be informed about the kind of congregation and task into which the new pastor is called.

I'm finding that the Scottdale congregation is unique, especially with its history of the denominational leadership via
the publishing ministry, and yet we are people who struggle
with the normal things of life: health, pain, conflict, family,
meaning, faith, and integrity. I am enjoying the challenge of
working within the current decline of the traditional congregation, yet with the hope that the rule of God is seeking new
forms at this major 500-year turn in history (Tickle).

I see great hope for Scottdale Mennonite Church as it engages its current circumstances and has leaders that want to
be more neighborhood-minded as we move into the future.
I see great hope for Scottdale Mennonite Church as it engages
its current circumstances and has leaders that want to be
more neighborhood-minded as we move into the future. In
fact, three congregational initiatives have developed over the
last year (2017–18) as the congregation moved into the task of
re-casting a vision and identity: 1) affirming and blessing the
work of first responders (fire, ambulance, police) through an
annual public recognition event—breakfast for first responders, fundraising on their behalf, conduit for anonymous
donors ($15,000 from an anonymous donor purchased 30
light-weight jumpsuits that were given to the top ten volunteers of three local fire stations in 2018), fire station open
house and prayer of blessing service; 2) creation care practical
engagement—the congregation became a member of the
Jacob's Creek Watershed Association (JCWA) and is helping
to raise awareness of environmental issues regarding the local
watershed, doing volunteer road and creek clean-up work,
getting to know others with creation-care vision by participating in JCWA hiking / creek events; 3) partnering with a
local pre-school / day care to help deliver high quality education and child care services to the local community—one of
our members has been assisting with accounting and book-

keeping, some others with maintenance and compliance issues, all of which may lead to selling, at less than market value, the former Kingview property to the group to help them establish a lasting footprint in the community.

These are examples of congregational discernment that is leading to a different kind of engagement between local congregation and community which may or may not produce membership increases, but what this congregation believes is taking incremental steps in forwarding God's kingdom outside our front door.

Dirk Kaufman said,

The Mennonite Church in Scottdale has long relied on a sense of mission, and that sense was sharpened by the coming in and going out of its congregants. For the past decade we have learned the challenge of staying still. We must learn which way to lean into standing from our stillness as we reach out to the community around us.

The challenge for the coming months and years is to retain a sense of who we are and how we got here while pushing that identity to a new place.

We know from our study and our day-to-day living that the church must be proactive and engage the culture that surrounds it. We will endeavor to both create a welcoming spirit and be prayerful in seeking how the Holy Spirit moves us in new directions. This is no small task, but we remain confident in the future of the church in small-town America.

As part of the effort to move ahead, the congregation adopted a Community Covenant for 2017–18. By early 2018 the covenant had been signed by 58 participants.

On November 11, 2017, the congregation voted to call David Mishler as half-time pastor for a three-year term.

Scottdale Mennonite Church Community Covenant 2017–2018

*B*ecause I attempt to make Jesus Christ the center of my life, with my sisters and brothers at Scottdale Mennonite Church:

I covenant to be a fervent seeker . . .
- following Jesus daily
- asking questions without fear

I will support the work of our congregation in seeking purpose and vision as we grow in faith and in support of each other in the coming year.

I covenant to demonstrate loving community . . .
- where all are welcome
- where all are needed

I will support a plan to identify ways to be relevant to our community, using what Spirit-given talents I have to assist as I am able.

I covenant to be a generous giver . . .
- money
- energy
- compassion
- time

I will give of myself and my gifts as I am able, undergirding all with prayer.

I covenant to be a bold dreamer . . .
- we are a work in process
- we will not be inhibited by human perceptions

I will join my sisters and brothers in dreaming new dreams and seeing new visions for ourselves and for our community, all under the guidance of the Holy Spirit.

_____   _____
Signature   Date

Will there be a Scottdale Mennonite Church in 2035? Will there be a Scottdale Presbyterian Church in 2035? Or two United Methodist churches?

Recently I read about a committee concerned about how to keep young people in our community. Employment opportunities are limited, but there are some. How can we keep young people in our community? And in our churches?

As described by Pastor David Mishler, our congregation is reaching out. Can we bring people in? Congregations are sometimes surprised by who appears. As reported in the October 8, 2018, issue of *Mennonite World Review*, Habecker Mennonite Church in Lancaster County, Pennsylvania, "decided to support a Karen refugee family from Myanmar, formerly known as Burma. The members' hospitality drew more Karen families. Ten years later, Karen people make up three quarters of Habecker's membership."

How this Habecker congregation will develop remains to be seen. Will Scottdale Mennonite experience a comparable infusion? We did welcome a Syrian family, but employment was limited, so the family went back to Syria with our blessing. More likely we will continue with and, we may hope, expand the vision we have amid Habecker-like openness to new possibilities.

What Happened to the Loucks Family?

A Closing Comment

by Daniel Hertzler

In *The Mennonites of Westmoreland County, Pennsylvania,* Edward Yoder reports that the Mennonite congregations here well-nigh collapsed in the nineteenth century. But they were revived in 1893 through the efforts of Aaron and Joseph Loucks.

This revival was celebrated in 1993 by the publication of a 30-page booklet. As I have noted in chapter 5 (above), Pastor John E. Sharp wrote about the 1893 renewal, which began with "a meeting [that] took place in the home of Jacob S. and Mary Saylor Loucks on July 22. Grandmother Nancy Stauffer Loucks (1808–1900), wife of the late minister Martin Loucks, is given credit for fanning the spark into flame."

With this kind of enthusiasm in the Loucks family, would we expect to find some Louckses in the Scottdale congregation today? There are none, although some continued until after the middle of the twentieth century. I found the record of their deaths in a congregational record book: Melinda Loucks, October 22, 1965; Jewell Loucks, December 29, 1975; Beulah Loucks, June 15, 1986. Jewell and his brother Don farmed land now owned by Woodcrest, a senior living community. The telephone directory lists eight people named Loucks living in or near Mount Pleasant and Greensburg. An article titled "Days Gone By" by Carol Westerman, in Scottdale's *Independent-Observer* for June 14, 2018, gives an example of how some of the Loucks family left the Mennonite Church.

She reports that Peter S. and Jacob S. Loucks were Mennonite farmers who "laid out the original plan for the town of Scottdale on a portion of the family farm. . . . They were both prominent in civic affairs. Moreover, Jacob was a leader in the Mennonite church, the family faith from which his four younger brothers departed."

Westerman draws from the memoirs of David Wendell Loucks, a grandson of Jacob S. Loucks. David writes with appreciation for his father and grandfather. David's father was a Mennonite but his mother a Presbyterian. "The Loucks families were Mennonites, and my father was active in the church there. But my mother never saw fit to join the church, and I think it was because she would have been obliged to wear the plain clothes prescribed by the church and enforced rigidly for women, and she could not bring herself to accept this."

He says that his father was a serious member and practitioner in the Mennonite church, but "Father never urged any of us or even suggested [that] we consider joining the Mennonite church."

The forward-looking statements by leaders of our congregation portray a vision for us to follow. They expect us to define more sharply who we are and the opportunities open to us. One thing we have accomplished, without necessarily planning for it, is to be open to people who find us a welcoming fellowship.

Among these have been Bryce and Becky King. He is a retired United Methodist minister, and we would not expect them to apply for membership, or to bring their daughter and grandchildren along since they live in Seattle. But Bryce has said that we are a "friendly church. We come together to meet each other's needs and go out to witness to other people." Bryce and Becky have moved right in and participate in the work and witness of the congregation. We are glad they are with us.

It would seem, however, that for long-term stability, a congregation should have multi-generations present: grandparents, parents, and grandchildren. We have only a few such families. Marty

Savanick and Jim and Linda Butti have grandchildren in our church. Who will carry the Anabaptist tradition into the future? It would not be reasonable to expect them to do it alone.

Anabaptists have often not been comfortable with the political context in which they live. Today in America, we live in an empire, although many churches seem less than aware of its implications and display the US flag in the meetinghouse. Theologians of other traditions than ours such as Walter Brueggemann, the late Walter Wink, Stanley Hauerwas, and William Willimon have all called attention to this problem, but it is not clear how many Christians are listening to them.

In the meantime, Anabaptism has spread around the world. *Rejoice* magazine published a June 17, 2018, prayer request for "the new Mennonite World Conference church, the Hmong Seventh District of the Church of Christ in Thailand, witnessing as a Hmong Christian minority group in a Buddhist culture among people of Chinese descent."

At the same time we hear that some wonder whether Mennonites will prevail in Holland, where there is a monument to Menno Simons and his assertion that there is no foundation other than Jesus Christ (1 Corinthians 3:11).

We may do well to remind ourselves that Jesus was not exactly a family man. Although it is reported that he was kind to children and cared about his mother, he apparently saw family systems in the way of the movement he was developing. Mark 3:33–35 reports that when his mother and brothers appear outside, he does not receive them. Indeed, in verse 35 he says, "Whoever does the will of God is my brother and sister and mother."

Throughout the centuries, churches have felt free to include whole families. But as illustrated by the Loucks family, we should not expect to rely on them alone. As Dirk Kaufman put it above, "We know from our study and our day-to-day living that the church must be proactive and engage the culture around it. We will endeavor to both create a welcoming spirit and be prayerful in seeking how the Holy Spirit moves us in new directions. This is no small task, but we remain confident in the future of the church in small-town America."

And, as I cannot resist adding, we need to affirm the declaration of Menno Simons rather than taking our theology from the U.S. Declaration of Independence.

Pastoral Reflection

by Donna Mast

WHEN I realized that God was inviting my husband and me to consider ministry at Kingview Mennonite Church in Scottdale, Pennsylvania, I thought God was playing some kind of joke on us. Then, after we had accepted the call from the Kingview congregation to fill their pastoral position, I told people that God certainly must have a sense of humor. My parents and paternal grandparents had been founding members of Kingview Mennonite Church. I was born while my family lived in Scottdale. When I was six years old, my parents moved to Ohio, and I considered Ohio to be my home.

One summer my husband and I traveled with our children to the area for a week of vacation at Laurelville Mennonite Church Center, near Mt. Pleasant, Pennsylvania. We were vacationing with friends. Between the two families, we had six little girls and had arranged for a tour of the Mennonite Publishing House. As my husband and I drove Pittsburgh Street, Scottdale, on the way to "The Pub," I told my husband, "I am so glad my parents chose to move away from here. I would never want to live here!"

About five years later we drove our moving van and car with family and stuff to Pennsylvania and moved into the house that would be our home for the next eighteen and a half years. I was sure God was laughing at me, but it was OK. I was laughing too. I was glad to be there.

While God may have been laughing, in looking back I am now absolutely certain that God gave us a gift in this call to serve in Scottdale. It was a privilege to live and serve in this community. Kingview Mennonite Church was a wonderful place in which to learn what it means to be a pastor. The congregation was gracious to us as we learned and allowed our children to just be children, not labeled "the pastors' kids." Later, when the financial crisis of publishing hit many in our congregation and in our sister congregation, Mennonite Church of Scottdale, we shed holy tears together as we prayed and tried to bring some comfort and hope to the community. People told us later that we helped to bring some stability to their shaking world. If this is true, it is by God's grace. A few years later, when it seemed best to gather up those who remained and join together as one congregation, it was amazing to see these faithful people, still wounded and hurting, come together to do this difficult thing of merging two congregations to become Scottdale Mennonite Church. It was certainly not easy, but I am blessed to have been a part of this particular portion of history.

The Mennonites of Scottdale are not perfect people. No one is! But they are faithful, generous, creative, and resilient. I know this from firsthand experience. I also saw these qualities in the lives of people who lived in Scottdale long before I was blessed to live there. I learned to know them through reading *On the Banks of Jacobs Creek*. Faithful people. People who are faithful to an even more faithful God. To God be the glory! ⋙

April 2018
Donna Mast
Pastor in Scottdale
from 1997 to 2011

Appendixes
Baptisms

THE lists of baptisms are drawn from bulletins and membership lists. Not listed here (with one exception) are other membership changes and transfers in and out, which appear in the church records now collected in the archives of Scottdale Mennonite Church.

Appendix 1
Baptisms for Mennonite Church of Scottdale

1940–2003

March 17, 1940. Charles Handlin Sr., Anna Handlin, Charles Handlin Jr., James Handlin, Dorothy Handlin, Samuel Cutrell

October 27, 1940. Leonard Brilhart, Carl Johnson

April 7, 1941. Harry Faust

May 4, 1941. Paul Yake, Carl Metzler, Mary Forsythe, Madeline Forsythe, Ray Forsythe Jr.

April 25, 1942. Floyd C. Brunk, Leota M. Brunk, Charles Hernley, Richard Dicks

November 7, 1942. Paul Stull

April 11, 1943. Virgil Yoder

May 20, 1944. Elizabeth Shoemaker, Ruth Cutrell, Gayle Millslagle, Stanley Yake, Paul Gamber, James Maust

November 4, 1944. Donald Eugene Brilhart, Donald Lee Brilhart, Richard Brilhart, John Stull, Erma Kauffman

May 5, 1945. Alice Marie Metzler

November 4, 1945. Joseph Alderfer, Paul Savanick

April 27, 1946. Vernon Hawk, Betty Ann Wenger

October 20, 1946. James Hawk, Viola Hawk

October 26, 1947. Louneta Etling, Thelma Hawk, Samuel McLean, Raymond McLean, Mary Albright

January 4, 1948. Mary Albright

March 14, 1948. Frederick Alderfer, Phyllis Lauver

September 12, 1948. Clifford Mast, Glenn Millslagle, Charles McLean, Byron Yake

April 24, 1949. James Sprinkle, John Horst Jr.

June 19, 1949. Washington Etling

October 30, 1949. Grace Wyse, Ivan Moon, Wendell Stants

April 9, 1950. Charlotte M. Millslagle

June 4, 1950. Rachel E. Horst, Alta Joyce Metzler, Abram J. Metzler, Lowell W. Shank, Anna Jane Stull, Edward Alderfer, Ivan Richard Keim, Fred Berg, Nancy Carol Sprinkle, Carol Millslagle, Norma Jean Geary, Blanche McLean, Margaret Ware, Mary Sidehamer

September 10, 1950. Mary McLean Geyer

December 10, 1950. James Alex Thomas

April 29, 1951. Mervin D. Zook, Merlin W. Zook, Mary Gayle Geary, Dorcas Elaine Hernley, Ruth Ann Brilhart, Morris Glen Mast, Ada Marie Mast, Sarah Louise Walsh, David K. Yoder, Larry R. Millslagle, Sandra Lee Michael, Dorothy Jane Stants, Anna Grace Lint

October 28, 1951. Bertha Fitzsimmons, William Fitzsimmons, Bertha Lee Hollis, Edward Richards

April 27, 1952. Rodney Hernley, Kenneth Plank, Charles Millslagle, Eugene Brilhart, Robert Brilhart

July 27, 1952. Phyllis Ann King (see the same date in Appendix 2)

October 26, 1952. Shirley Ann Vernon, Druscilla Jean Rankin, Jean Goshorn, Mary Goshorn

October 4, 1953. Nina Leanne Stull, Clark Albright

December 6, 1953. Daniel Lind, Lowell Hebenthal, Elva Rae Hebenthal, Ronald Vernon, James DeWalt

August 29, 1954. Elmer Hawk, Sanford Plank, Philip Shank, James Alderfer

June 6, 1954. William Worry

February 20, 1955. David Francis McLean, Martha E. Lint, Freda Yvonne Walsh, Vivian Ruth Walsh

July 3, 1955. Florina Walters

April 28, 1957. Ellen Elizabeth Hernley, Grace Ann Michael, Penny Lee Yoder

August 25, 1957. Minnie Hawk

September 22, 1957. Rachel Stants, Kathleen Stants

October 27, 1957. Robert Wenger

December 25, 1958. Marilyn Hernley

May 3, 1959. Ruth Ann Bender, Janet Brenneman, Judy Brenneman, Lorraine Byer, Eli Savanick, Rosetta Savanick, Dorothy Shank, Lowell Stull, Lois Stull, Steve Yoder

April 17, 1960. James Cutrell, Hesston Lauver, Anita Hartzler, Ruby Plank, Carol Shank, Barbara Yoder

April 30, 1961. Keith Millslagle, Wayne Millslagle, Barry Christner, Reuben Savanick, David J. Fisher.

August 13, 1961. Carole Brilhart

March 25, 1962. Joan Byer, Larry Shetler

August 25, 1963. Goldie Plank, Jon Cutrell

November 1, 1964. Kenneth Hartzler, Stephen Shank, David Cutrell, Kathleen (Stull) Smoker, Theodore Brilhart

June 12, 1966. Roger Hernley

August 7, 1966. Wayne Royer

October 23, 1966. Julia Fisher, Suzette Fisher, James Lederach, Judith Lederach, Diane Yoder, Sally Kauffman

December 24, 1967. Linda Byer, Tim Abel Jr., Kathleen Brilhart, Ellen Millslagle, Tom Yoder, Betty Shank

December 31, 1968. Elsa Savanick

September 28, 1969. Ray Ramos, Beverly Ramos

October 3, 1971. Louis Kritz, Lorraine Kritz

May 28, 1972. Daniel Brilhart, Lowell Fisher, Anthony Horsch, Debbie Lederach, Cindy Shetler, Jerri Studer, Debbie Willard, Janice Yoder

March 11, 1973. Dolores Frick, Patty Frick, Bill Frick, Jennifer Yoder, Chris Reist, Francine Kaiser

November 17, 1974. Teresa Dal Moulin

December 8, 1974. Kenton Beachy, Jenny Cressman, Janet Horsch, Marcella Hostetler, Rebecca Lederach, Kenneth Millslagle, Terry Paul, James Spicher

December 15, 1974. Luiz Dal Moulin

January 5, 1975. Wendy Ware

March 9, 1975. David Mayercheck, Kathleen Francis Mayercheck

June 8, 1975. Jeffrey Millslagle

May 23, 1976. Laura Brubaker, Julia Spicher, Diane Kolb

June 27, 1976. Carl Pritchard

January 16, 1977. Monica Hostetler

January 29, 1978. Linda Paul, Gregory Millslagle

January 21, 1979. Jim Wion

April 8, 1979. Audrey Brubaker, Craig Shetler

April 29, 1979. Pam Walker, Robert Walker

September 2, 1979. Linda Jo Gleysteen

November 23, 1980. Michael Cressman

January 3, 1982. DiAnna Kay Cooper, Jon Horsch, Jefferson Spicher

August 1, 1982. Robin Barkley LaFranchise, Amy Brubaker, Amy Frey Salch, Heather Martin Gillespie

November 27, 1983. Dan Neiderhiser

April 22, 1984. Dale Hartzler

July 1, 1984. Sherilyn Bentz

October 7, 1984. John Johnson

November 11, 1984. Jeffrey Shetler

July 28, 1985. Max Bentz, Denver Sommers, Tom Zeller

August 24, 1986. Bruce Campbell, Marlene Campbell

July 10, 1988. David Cooper, Dickson Sommers

October 2, 1988. Louise Dunston Lederach, William Gratchic, Joseph Green, Brenda Johnson

August 23, 1992. Melanie Green

June 12, 1994. Deborah Millslagle

February 5, 1995. André Kalend

August 13, 1995. Gail Butti, Joe E. Green III, Nicole Heller, Caleb Johnson, Ben Savanick, Nathan Savanick, Erin Sharp, M. J. Sharp, Nathan Sprunger

November 26, 1995. Michael James Butti, Andrew Wayne Hurst, Rachel Ellyn Sprunger

December 21, 1997. Margaret Fox, Molly Hurst, Dirk Kaufman, Mary Kaufman, Hallie Pritts

April 4, 1999. Adam Savanick, Matthew Sprunger, Vetha Stull, Melanie Walker Whirlow

April 23, 2000. Dale Smith, Charmaine Smith, Sam Zehr, Julia Zehr, Emily Millslagle

December 31, 2000. Julian Johnson

April 15, 2001. James Zaronsky, Christopher Pritts

April 27, 2003. Mindy L. Evans

Appendix 2

Baptisms for Kingview

1952–2003

July 27, 1952. Robert Welty, Ruby Fern Vernon, Verna Maxine Vernon, Wilma Louise Vernon (all baptized at Scottdale for Kingview)

October 26, 1952. Druscilla Rankin, Shirley Vernon, Jean Goshorn, Mary Lou Goshorn (all baptized at Scottdale for Kingview)

December 6, 1953. New members received by transfer or confession of faith (baptized elsewhere): Ronald Vernon, Elva Rae Hebenthal, Lowell Hebenthal, James DeWalt, Mildred Swank, Daniel Lind

April 10, 1960. Dan Alderfer, Eric Alderfer, Jonathan Lind, Joseph Slabaugh, Michael Slabaugh

June 14, 1964. Olgie Green

January 8, 1967. Dennis Hertzler, Alan Yoder

February 18, 1968. Arlene Green, Valerie Green, Herbert Green Jr.

April 6, 1969. Herbert Green Sr., Bill Swank Sr.

May 17, 1970. Dan Mark Hertzler, Nathan Yoder, Peter Waybill, Dave Yoder, Dirk Miller, Gregory Paul, Kim Miller, Ronald Drescher, Beverly Myers, Kim Groce, Sandra Drescher, Debbie Swartzentruber, Rosie Drescher, Emily Miller, Julia Swartzentruber, Ann Yoder, Carmen Schrock, Rachel Moon

October, 22, 1971. Lou Forsythe

May 7, 1972. Yvonne Stull, Edith Kropp

June 4, 1972. Joyce Stokes

October 29, 1972. Carol Roadman

August 26, 1973. Roger Stokes, Ronald Hertzler, Gerald Hertzler

February 3, 1974. Lisa Eicher, Lois Moon, Tim Sprinkle, Judy Swank

July 6, 1975. Billy Swank Jr., Sue Swank

May 16, 1976. Ann Miller, Joyce Myers, Andrea Schrock, Brent Schrock, Jean Swartzentruber, John Swartzentruber, Lois Waybill

June 5, 1977. Marlene Schwab

May 21, 1978. John Schwab

January 3, 1982. Randall Ledyard

December 12, 1982. Bill and Alta Dezort

April 3, 1983. Toni Brown, Roland Ledyard, Mark Keyser, Steven Krall, Jon Peachey, Laura Roth, Traci Sprinkle, Becky Waybill, Susan Weaver

March 20, 1988. Don Echard

August 28, 1988. Steve Cavanaugh, Kim Bialek

June 4, 1989. Rachel Brubacher, Amy Martin, Bob Swank

December 10, 1989. Charles Lint

July 28, 1990. Les and Pam Philburn

January 31, 1993. Barbara Hollenbaugh

April 4, 1993. Hannah Miller

October 17, 1993. Elaine Swank

May 31, 1998. Susan Bucar, Philip Clausner, Mary Hughes, Katie Mast, Samantha Peterson, Jason Yoder

March 19, 2000. Celebration of baptism and reception of new members. No names given

June 10, 2001. Daniel Stutzman

June 9, 2002. Kathy Stutzman, Katie Meyer

May 11, 2003. Bulletin report: Four young persons to be baptized on June 8 after merger between Kingview Mennonite and the Mennonite Church of Scottdale. See Appendix 4

Appendix 3
Baptisms for North Scottdale
1959–1969

NORTH SCOTTDALE was organized as a separate congregation on May 3, 1959. Before that applicants were baptized at the Mennonite Church of Scottdale and appear in Appendix 1.

April 3, 1960. Ann Alderfer, Joe Brenneman, David Hershberger, Deborah Hershberger, Priscilla Hershberger, Louise Shank, Jerry Sprinkle

September 20, 1964. Lois Miller

April 18, 1965. Charles Bender, Barbara Paul, Norma Shank

October 23, 1966. Daniel Lint, Homer Walters

June 4, 1967. Faith Alderfer, Roger Paul, Russell Smoker, Rodney Sprinkle, Gale Walters

April 20, 1969. Philip Paul

Appendix 4

Baptisms for Scottdale Mennonite Church after Merger in 2003

June 8, 2003. Mark Johnson, Leah Rittenhouse, Annika Miller, Anna Weaver

October 2, 2005. James Lederach, Krista Rittenhouse

January 13, 2008. Josiah Hartzler, Joshua Millslagle, Grace Weaver, Justin Hernley

July 14, 2013. Rachel Bryner (by immersion in Jacobs Creek)

The Author

VIRGIL YODER

DANIEL HERTZLER moved to Scottdale in 1952 to work at Mennonite
Publishing House. He and his wife,
Mary, became members of Kingview
Mennonite Church when it was organized in 1955. They transferred to
the merged Scottdale Mennonite
congregation in 2003. Dan retired
from Mennonite Publishing House
in 1990, after being editor of *Gospel
Herald* since 1973.

Dan served in the local church-
es, Allegheny Mennonite Conference, and certain educational responsibilities with the churchwide Mennonite organizations. (See
chapter 4 in *On My Way*.) He retired in 2015 as director of Unit 2 in
Pastoral Studies Distance Education for Anabaptist Mennonite
Seminary.

Daniel Hertzler is the author of two memoirs: *A Little Left of
Center* (Pandora Press U.S., now Cascadia, 2000) and *On My Way*
(Cascadia, 2013). Both are available from Cascadia Publishing
House, Telford, Pennsylvania.

www.ingramcontent.com/pod-product-compliance
Lightning Source LLC
Chambersburg PA
CBHW022009080426
42733CB00007B/532